TOXIC AMERICA

Essays

J.D. Gill, Ph.D.

KDP
2020

BOOKS BY J.D. GILL

FORMS OF LIFE and other essays
LETTERS TO JIM
FINDING HUMAN
LETTERS OF JULIET to the Knight in Rusty Armor
ONE HUNDRED REASONS WHY I LOVE YOU
THE MISERY OF THE GOOD CHILD
CIRCUMFERENCE A memoir
IN BETWEEN Poems 1964 - 1996
RECURRING THEMES IN THE TAROT AND THE SELF
MEXICO PAPERS VOLS 1 - 3
SEEING in Intimacy and Psychotherapy
SILENCE AT THE CENTER OF TIME: Essays
ROME FIRST: Journeys of the Self
LOVE LASTS FOREVER: Beyond Circumference
POEMS VOLUME TWO
POEMS VOLUME THREE

I think that to overcome regionalism, you must have a great deal of self-knowledge. I think that to know yourself is to know the world, and in a sense, paradoxically, it's also to be an exile from that world. So that you have a great deal of detachment.

—Flannery O'Connor

CONTENTS

TOXIC AMERICA

In the developmental process it is important that reality be introduced to the infant slowly, in steps the infant can accommodate. If reality is introduced too rapidly, the infant is overwhelmed and faces an alien situation without the necessary tools to cope.

Initially the infant's frame or context includes itself and whatever directly pertains to itself. The infant can optimally reach out to elements in this context only if those elements are felt to be safe, and the infant feels welcome among them. In other words, right at the start, the infant learns either the world is a safe and welcoming place or an unsafe and unwelcoming place.

Also when the external surround is safe and welcoming the infant is able to be interested in both the internal and external space. The infant is said to have good contact with reality.

When the external surround is frightening or unwelcoming, the infant must seek solace in his or her interior space, i.e., the self. When my occupation is primarily with the self, I am said to be narcissistic.

Klein (see Hinshelwood and Fortuna, 2017) and Fairbairn (1994) (see also Riviera, 2017) famously tried to account for how a newborn is able to maintain attachment to his or her mother. This is a problem, because the mother is not a perfectly rewarding presence. Sometimes she is not rewarding or is even frustrating. Things that are rewarding are good, whereas things that are not rewarding are bad. Thus the child develops a good image of the mother and a bad image. It was thought the infant retains the good image and projects the bad image. Since the attachment is now to the good mother, it may persist. Also, since the bad image has been projected outside of the self, the self can also see itself as a good entity.

The only problem with this arrangement is that the bad, now located in frustrating elements outside the self, might pose a danger to the self. It is therefore something to be feared. Nonetheless, such a development allows for the infant's first successful adjustment.

In other words a well-adjusted infant will be able to find safety and welcome both within him or herself and (within developmental limits) in the outside world. Again if it isn't safe in the outside world, the infant retreats to the inside world.

For example, if I think I am wonderful, but those around me think I am a liability, the (as it were) inside view is preferable to the outside view.

Part of the reason this is the case is that the inside view is importantly under my control in a way the outside world, or elements in the outside world, is not. Focus on my own viewpoint turns the focus inward. This allows me to modify internal elements to support a positive view of myself. It also allows me to be able to relocate (project) bad elements out of myself onto the outside world. In this way I can feel I am good, but the world is not.

With increasing development I am able to realize that both the good image (object) and the bad image (object) are within me. I am both good and bad, and this is true of other people as well.

Failure in this system may be the result of inadequate or abusive parenting. For example, my mother may feel the good element is within her, and the bad element is within me. I may be taught I am a bad kid.

The above logic has been used to account for what has been called "toxic masculinity." Here, it is thought the person has experienced an inadequacy or problem in himself. In order to keep this inadequacy or problem from being known by others who he feels will therefore react negatively, he counters it by displaying a hyper-strong image to others. Thus the hyper-strong image protects the inadequate feeling from being known. In other words, instead of resolving the interior feeling, a competing image is displayed.

The resulting displayed image is unable to admit of any weakness. (It is weakness it is trying to deny.) The self must be ascendant and unquestionable.

Such an organization may be the result of what Lakoff (2009, 2016) has called the Strict Father Family. Here, father issues demands, and the family obeys. Failures to obey are punished with force in order to maintain the father's position in the autocratic structure.

It is easy to see that families are not the only institutions structured in this way. Many businesses, governments, schools, police departments, armies, religions, &c. are also similarly constituted. In all these cases, when things go the leader's way, they are considered good. When they do not go the leader's way, they are considered bad.

Such a structure in inherently weak in that it is set up to resist new ideas and growth. Since the person in question must be in charge—and admit to no weakness—all ideas deemed to be of worth must come from him. If there is a good idea that comes from someone else, it threatens the system.

This is why the person in question surrounds himself with yes-men, people who reflect back to him how wonderful he is. Anything else would be threatening and is thus avoided. When the only thing a person can tolerate or hear is agreement, he is doomed to live inside a prison of his own construction.

Strength, however, is not the only element that can be seen to operate in this way. Almost any sort of superiority can function in a similar fashion. That is, an image of superiority can be used to hide feelings of inadequacy. Often, when this is the case, the superiority is exaggerated.

There can be no breach in the armor. Strength, superiority, talent, and/or prowess must be displayed to the last breath in order to successfully mask the inferiority that is hiding behind it. As the TV commercial says: "Never let them see you sweat."

The resultant artificial person is deprived of natural spontaneity, nuance, and the ability to be intimate. These are dangerous elements with regard to the maintenance of the strong and capable facade. Being wrong about something is not routine at all. It is a four-alarm fire.

An infant raised in a nurturing parent family is, on the other hand, able to find safety both in him or herself and also in the outside surround. A large part of why this is so is that the infant is able to find him or herself reflected in the minds of others. In other words, the (significant) others in his or her life are concerned with the infant's feelings.

When one's feelings matter and are accepted, one feels safe. It is when one's feelings cannot be taken into account that one feels unsafe.

It is for this reason a child in a nurturing parent family finds the emphasis is placed on how people feel as well as what they think. A child in a strict father family finds the emphasis is placed on behavior (i.e., following the rules).

Obviously these two children are drawn in stereotypical fashion to make a point. It is nevertheless true that all children tend along a continuum from one pole to the other.

Important in each of these cases is an unconscious or preconscious awareness of the context or frame in which the family exists. That is, unless learned otherwise, the child will assume the world is essentially like the context or frame of the family in which he or she developed. In other words, things are seen in the world the way they were seen at home.

The world will either seem interested in how I feel and think, or it will seem interested in how I behave. I will feel as safe and welcome in the world as I did at home. In this way the world will appear either welcoming or unwelcoming.

I will also tend to gravitate toward those groups that feel as I do and who see the world as I do. There will be comfort in these numbers. If the world is unsafe, the group must focus on protection. If the world is welcoming the group may seek to contribute to it.

If the world is dangerous it will be important to identify people who are with us (on our side) and those who are not with us—or against us. *We* will be the good group, and *they* will be the bad group. We will be right, and they will be wrong. We will seek to strengthen our position against them.

Banding together in the cause of being ascentant will further protect us from the feelings of inadequacy we hide under our external stance. We will reinforce each other. It is in this way groups can function somewhat as individuals and have similar qualities.

America is often described as a narcissistic culture. The most impressive buildings in America are not the buildings of state, the schools, or the churches. The most impressive buildings are the banks. This is, it is said, what we value: wealth and power. Close by the banks are buildings of corporations and businesses whose goal it is to accrue more wealth and power.

Further, we are largely focused on ourselves. A huge segment of the world doesn't have enough to eat, but we feel that is not our problem. Wars, unless they involve us, are not of central importance. We want to get ahead and stay ahead. It is about us. As a rule we don't speak other languages.

This characterization is truer of the strict father group than it is of the nurturing parent group. In the strict father group the struggle for ascendency has a defensive quality. Here it is *necessary* that one be ascendant to protect against disallowed feelings of inadequacy. One's identity is at stake.

No one wants to belong to an inferior group, school, religion, race, or gender. No one wants to be an outsider. We want to belong—and belong to the best group. We want to be on top. Who wouldn't?

This is why your group, school, political party, religion, race, gender, line of work, &c. is inferior to mine. Being better is best, as any fool knows. Soon we find ourselves involved in what Freud called the "narcissism of small differences." My ball-point pen is better than yours.

The circle is closed when being the best becomes more important than the qualities that actually make something what it is. That is, it is not the best because of its merits; it is the best because we say it is.

II

What is important to note about this situation is that power often inheres in the ability to define the context or the frame in which elements will be considered. Defining the frame is to define the field of play.

My parents could have defined the frame as my family alone. They could have defined the frame as the entire world. The frame constitutes the range of things that matter. My parents may also have taught that things within the frame are good, and things outside the frame are bad.

If, for example, I live in a small town there may be an assumption that this town and the way things are done and valued here is the way things *should* be. What is done and valued elsewhere is erroneous or wanting.

The frame becomes the small town along with the attitudes and values it has. Other attitudes and values are not as important if not wrong and/or dangerous. Such a situation is a bit like the old maps of the world that held it was flat—that if one were to sail too far away, one would fall off the edge.

Besides, in this town we all agree as to what is right and wrong. Our values are the right ones, and we know what is best in life. Our religion is the right one, and others are wrong. Why would anyone want to move away? Moving away is simply to move *down* to a lesser place. Besides not being able to learn much about the "outside world" (other than it is wrong, inferior, &c.), townspeople have no ability to deal with it. One only knows how to deal with the town.

I would be lost in a big city. No one would know who I am, and the way they do things would be strange. I had some stature in the small town, but here I am unknown. I have never been taught, nor have I ever learned how, to deal with a frame such as this. If I stay, it will be a difficult transition.

If I do stay for a while and begin to develop contacts, have work or school tasks to accomplish, and begin to know my way around, I will be learning and operating in a different frame from that of the small town. If, at this point, I return to the small town for a visit, I may find my efforts in the new context devalued the old context. "Who would want to live in a place like that?" The only things of value are what happen in the small town.

I may be forced to toggle between frames. Having now experienced more than one frame, I am able to see the small town as well as the city from both the inside and the outside.

This ability is not to be understated. It is critical to the development of a less limited world view. Experiencing different contexts allows me to see them in relation to others. That is, I can see where one context lies (as well as where it does not) in the greater frame of all contexts. In this sense knowledge is comprised of *breadth* as well as *depth*.

It is a tenant of postmodernism (Lyotard (1984), Foucault (1970), et al. that what one sees depends upon where one stands. That is, the act of seeing itself is partially constitutive of the experience (Heideger, 1949). The frame of reference of the subject is involved in the perception of the object. A neutral subject (whatever that may be) is impossible.

I may be in a position to compare frames or contexts. Which one ranks higher according to some set of criteria?

Which one offers the most opportunity, the most relaxation, &c.

Such a comparison need not become a "king of Bunker Hill" sort of affair where the loudest and most forceful prevails. Nor is it the case that reality is a composition of accidental frames—though the perception of it may well be. Epistemologically speaking what is common to all frames is language.

A street in the small town is the same sort of thing as it is in the city. What significance it may have for one or the other of us may be different, but the word is not used differently in either case. If I call the street a chair, I have misused the language (unless there is some game involved). A street is a street. If that were not the case, no frame would be possible as "the world" would be an incoherent jumble (See Wittgenstein 1953, Gadamer, 1989, et al).

This is to say that language is the great uhr-frame (transcendent frame).

The choice of frame in any given situation will likely fall to power unless there is a search for the most inclusive frame, the most detailed frame, the frame with the most utility in a given situation, &c.

We live in a culture in which there are constant battles over which frame we should be using. Once the frame is wittingly or unwittingly agreed upon (joined), the outcome is easier to see. When the frame cannot be agreed upon, we remain splintered apart.

When the frame is used to define a field of study, advancements will take place within that frame. Advancements outside the frame may well be ignored. These outside views may be stated in unfamiliar terms, based on unclear criteria, and may be the result of different logical uses. In a great many cases, knowledge will remain within the frame just as experience remains within the frame of the small town.

Just as an advanced frame is required to appreciate modern painting or poetry, a more advanced frame is required to appreciate psychoanalysis or the "great attractor" of chaos theory. As our knowledge and awareness expands, the frame is able to widen as well as deepen.

III

We live in a culture in which great numbers of people are poor, uneducated, suffering, living under crippling psychological stress, and who live in restricted contexts. Others of us have everything we want. We are educated, solvent, well-traveled and are able to consider multiple contexts.

All of us are Americans. We have yet to find a way to make each of us feel included let alone feel safe and welcome. Caught up in issues of disparate frames, our efforts tend to bypass each other—and we are more comfortable with people who are like us than with anyone else.

I used to laugh that my Los Angeles friends would say to me, "*Why* do you live in Utah?" My Salt Lake City friends would say, "You *like* Los Angeles?"

Surely an essential element in our dilemma lies in the fact that so many of us feel inadequate in our own lives. We are the product of families that were unable to help us accommodate well to reality and, at the same time, feel worthwhile. So we had to invent or piece together whatever esteem we have. Everyone else seemed to have it, and we didn't want (shudder) to be less than them.

Before one is able to drop his or her constructed or superior image, that person must experience many things including: meaningful resonance with another person, being valued simply for who one is (a person), being accepted as an equal, and a context of safety. Until these things happen, forget it.

In Strict Father Families the thoughts and feelings of children do not exist in a context where they are safe and welcome. The emphasis is not on *who* you are but on *how* you behave or how much you accomplish. Who you are, including how you think and feel, doesn't matter. Power is what matters.

When it is power that matters, primitive aspects of psychology come into play. A society based on power is a primitive society. In contrast, a society based on nurturing is a humane society.

Lakoff (Ibid) described the power grid as follows:

...the Disciplined (Strong) against the Undisciplined (Weak), the Rich above the Poor, Employers above Employees, Adults above Children, Western culture above other cultures, America above other countries. The hierarchy extends to: Men above Women, Whites above Nonwhites, Christians above Non-Christians, Straights above Gays.

When this is the enforced order, personal development suffers—*even if* you are a member of the privileged class. This is so as you are required to be something you are not just as members of an underprivileged class are required to be something they are not. Both are required to have a value that is assigned by the frame instead of having value inherent in themselves (see Baldwin 1972, Coates, 2015).

Such an order weakens the whole and renders it defensive. This situation occurs, because people have been assigned roles in the frame instead of being encouraged to find out who they truly are and how to value and be that person. The result is a society of images or constructions, each one working overtime to maintain its own effect.

If a White person must be superior to a Black person, neither of them is allowed to be real. The same is true for the categories of men and women, rich and poor, &c. Outside a specific frame of reference such distinctions make no sense. The privileged and the poor are both categories in the frame—and defined by the frame. What is considered privileged in one place may not be so considered in another.

What such categories and images create, however, is a way for people to hide their own reality behind them. Thus I may be wealthy but a terrible person. When the frame is humanity instead of a particular society, the picture may look quite different.

Categories and images also may serve to distort perceptions. I may see White people differently from Black people. I may consider rich people to be constitutionally different from poor people. I may attribute to them different significance and humanity. The category to which they belong may comprise the entirety of my sense of them. That is I may neglect to look beyond the categories and images to try to find the real persons involved.

In such fashion whole groups can appear to be categories and images—with no genuine people behind them. This is a way to dehumanize people into characterizations. Such a process is dangerous as it dramatically increases the potential for abuse.

Alterity is a process that has three steps. One: I draw a distinction between myself and *others.* Two: I place (project) the parts of myself I don't want to acknowledge onto the others. Three: This system is institutionalized.

When I draw a distinction between myself and others, I characterize myself as an individual and others as a group. Thus I strip others of their individuality. They are all considered to be similar. When I project my bad parts onto them, I arrange it so I am good, and they are bad. Thus I debase them. When this action becomes a family, group, or social norm, then it is considered to be reality.

All of these activities take place within a frame or context. The frame is important. It contains what we can know and to a large degree what we can see. The frame shapes the kind of life we are able to have.

IV

A few years ago I was visiting the island of Crete. Somewhere during my travels I lost my passport. When I discovered this I went to the tourist bureau in Heraklion and explained the situation. I was told there was no American Embassy on Crete, so I would have to go to Athens. I went to the airport and found I could fly to Athens, but I could not leave Greece.

Early the next morning I flew to Athens and found myself in a near-empty airport. I could find no information desk, and I felt very lost and alone indeed. Finally I noticed a kiosk open that advertised travel. I asked the lady at the counter if she could find me a hotel in Athens. "Yes," she replied. Where in the city did I want to stay? "The Plaka" I told her, having been to Athens twice before. She phoned several numbers and then told me, "I found a hotel that has a room for one night only." I took it, she gave me a paper to give the taxi driver, and I was on my way.

The taxi took me to the wrong hotel, but the desk man was understanding and drew the route to my hotel on a map. I arrived at my hotel and checked in. I then asked the desk crew if they knew where the American Embassy was. They did and drew the route on another map. I was to take the subway.

I arrived at the American Embassy, cleared the extensive security and approached the passport window. I explained I had lost my passport. The lady behind the window then asked me a question I had never heard before: "Do you have any proof you are a U.S. citizen?"

Do you have any proof of who you are?

I had a driver license and a photocopy of my passport. I handed them over, and she told me to take a seat. As I sat there the significance of the context fell over me. Outside the frame in which I was known, who was I? How was I different from anyone else? Without papers, I was just another person on the hot sidewalk. Shorn of context, I was simply myself. No one knew me.

We are each creatures of a context. It is within those contexts we live and are known. Outside the context we have no dimension, because we have not established one. In an important sense, we are a nobody. It is a precarious feeling indeed.

The embassy eventually issued me a replacement passport, I collected my belongings from security, and returned to the street. This time I felt much better. I was somebody. I had a passport to prove it. I would be allowed to return home.

V

Many of us have been raised in homes where we were taken to doctors, dentists, churches, and schools—but we were never taken to therapists. Nor had our parents ever consulted a therapist. Psychotherapy was outside the frame in which the family functioned. For many of us it was our parents who were the authorities. And where did they get the knowledge they had? Often it was from their parents who also didn't consult therapists and also from acquaintances in their lives.

Health care issues they had were often referred to professionals or relevant literature. But psychology remained beyond this horizon. Consequently, our parents responded as if they knew what to do whether or not they actually did. We learned this is how it is done. Our parents were the captains of the ship, and they were to be honored and obeyed. They could be idiots, but they still deserved our undying allegiance.

If we were lucky we had parents who helped us figure out who we are. They listened to us, and we listened to them. The goal was to help us feel good about ourselves and others—and how to function in the world. If we were unlucky we had parents who taught us a correct way to behave and punished us when we did not do this. We did it their way, because they said so. That was, they said, reason enough.

They also said society in general held the same views they did. How they knew this was a mystery as they had not experienced very much of society. We felt alone and doomed, because it was not allowed for us to feel angry. But we were angry, and we were never taught a way to deal with anger in a healthy way. We stuffed it, or acted it out, or grew up to direct it against those who do not conform to what we think is right.

If we ever did consult a therapist we expected that person to tell us what to do—the right thing to do. We expected, that is, such a person to be like our parents. We expected them to have the right answer for us. That's what they are for, isn't it?

In this way arrogance, blindness, and damage is passed along without any check. "It was good enough for my mother, so it's good enough for me." "Kids are too coddled nowadays anyway."

All such children hear at home, in church, at school is how to behave. No one asks, "What do you think?" "How do you feel?" Answers to these questions would likely be corrected anyway as they would not agree with the one asking. In a real sense these children have been abandoned. They have been shaped into behaviorisms in a world of right and wrong.

When they get to high school the pressure to fit in will be brutal. Those who do not fit the established norm are thrown away. Where, one might ask, did all of these young people learn to behave in such a way? How could they be so inhumane? The answer is: they were raised this way.

Soon after high school many of them will start their own families, and what will they use as guidance? Understanding therapists?

We may say such a system rests on parental abuse of authority. The parents, who in no way are experts, set themselves up as experts and seek control by means of intimidation. Their children either comply or rebel. Sometimes they just freeze with fear—and then cover this fear with substance abuse.

When these young people get a job, they are expected to comply with directives and performance guidelines. *This is all they are required to do.* They need not be complete persons who are able to function in psychologically healthy ways. If there is a problem, it will likely be related to the following of guidelines.

It becomes a whole life of following rules. Whether or not one is also a developed person is not considered.

When this scenario is duplicated millions of times, in millions of homes and millions of jobs, a society is formed that doesn't know who it is. If society is a reflection of the people who make it up, that society will be one that struggles with thinking and feeling. Its cities will be good at logistics but not very warm.

And it will not be very open to psychotherapy or insight into its issues. The culture, being a reflection of the people who make it up, will not respond well to being challenged—no matter how carefully this is done. When such a pattern is the frame of the culture, it is far from healthy.

Mental health and a fulfilling life are supposed to just happen or to be claimed in spite of the truth. Power is not to be questioned. On the contrary, it is to be defended to the last person. This sort of power is toxic.

Tyranny is based on narcissism. The tyrant seeks to replace the natural order with his or her own order where the tyrant is in control. This control is maintained by power instead of understanding and mental health. The goal of such an order is to maximize the return to the tyrant. It is not to maximize the good of those subject to the order.

When power is the operative element instead of health, concerns about well-being tend to fall by the wayside. The focus is on, say, how big the corporation can become. In this pursuit, the corporation pits itself in opposition to everything else.

The human need to feel worthwhile may be universal, but it is not a zero-sum game. That is, my feeling worthwhile does not depend on you feeling worthless. If there can only be a few people who are okay, the system is not widely beneficial. And it is even worse if those not okay have to be miserable.

For this reason a healthy society requires a different concept of power. This requires focusing on awareness instead of force. The difference is between pushing people around versus enlightening them with an awareness of who they are (and who they are not). That is the less authoritarian and more informed a society becomes the more humane it also becomes. Such a move allows awareness to be brought to a larger group in contrast to allowing only one or a few to be able to wield force. If the actions of the one or few must be agreed upon by the larger group, power tends to shift.

This is not an argument for utopia. Through our greatest efforts we will not succeed in creating a world in which tyranny is eradicated. But we can reduce the number of tyrants. We can reduce it in ourselves and our families if nowhere else.

Even so such efforts still will not eliminate the psychological damage that gives rise to the lust for power as that lies beyond our current capabilities. Increasing awareness of healthy family, work, and school systems, however, might be more widely achieved and is worth attempting.

A culture is only as healthy as its constituent members. Increased knowledge of childhood attachment, the psychodynamics of personality structure, &c. is easily as important as information about balanced diets and immu-

nization. This requires trained therapists to be added into
the mix of the family's health care contacts.

Just as there is a considerable difference between people who have had children and those who have not—or
those who have gone to college and those who have not
—so there is considerable difference between people who
have experienced their own psychotherapy and those who
have not. It is a difference in perspective hard to achieve
any other way. It is a difference in perspective our society sorely requires.

VI

In most cases your auto insurance company doesn't
want to fix your car adequately. It wants to fix it cheaply.
The cheaper the better. Your health insurance plan, if it
covers your issue at all, demands stifling mountains of
paperwork that digitalize and compromise your care.
Your computer feeds are tailored to your previous internet
searches, so you only receive a certain portion of what is
available. Companies scan your data to find out which
stores you frequent, what newspapers you read, what political parties and religious organizations you follow.

Commodities are made by companies seeking to maximize profit instead of quality. There is a science of doing
this. There are not enough teachers, policemen, or doctors. Everything you get is minimized so what they get is
maximized. And who are they?

They are the ones who make a profit from what you buy, how you spend your time, how you eat, dress, what you read, and where you go. The system is geared toward profit. This in itself may not be a problem. It becomes one when self-focus and greed enters the picture.

This brings us back to power and inadequacy. How much does one really need? An answer to this depends upon what sort of lack one is seeking to correct.

Internal deficits are constantly being compensated for by external means. If I feel worthless, I at least can have a fancy car. I need the fancy car to feel I am better than I know (at some level) I am. I want more. In fact, there is no end to what I want. Even though what I have now doesn't make my life meaningful, I feel a little more will. Besides I need to keep up with the neighbors. I don't want to be thought inadequate.

Soon plunder enters the equation. I demand people accord me my due. I will do anything to increase my standing. I exploit those who work for me, driving them to unrealistic performance levels so I can have more. The labels in my clothes matter. Someone might look. I want them to be impressed.

It is the *demand* that makes it pathological.

It seems everyone is after the same thing. This requires me to work harder and to gain more. More is better. When I die, I want people to be amazed at how much I was able to amass. My success will be my glory. It will not be who I really am. It will not be how considerate I was. It will not be whether or not I was able to help any-one. No. My glory will be in my power.

Caught in an endless competitive loop, I am unable to think much about the welfare or plight of others. I am too busy thinking about my own plight and welfare. Besides I can't help others do better. No one helps me.

But they do.

They pave my streets, filter my water, guard my neighborhood, stock the shelves at my grocery, grade the papers of my children, provide my entertainment, and care for me when I am ill. What would it take for me to be able to look these people in the eye and feel kinship?

It would require the opposite of alterity. It would require me to think of all of us as standing together instead of apart. This is one thing narcissistic individuals fear: being ordinary. It an insult to be ordinary. The only way to be okay is to be special, better than others. Narcissistic individuals don't have enough ego strength to allow themselves to be ordinary. Ordinary is too close to feelings of inadequacy. Superior is much better. The only way such a person can feel okay about him or herself is to have more.

In Franny and Zooey, Salinger wrote: I'm sick of not having the courage to be an absolute nobody.

Culture is thus torn apart by a need to compensate for a perceived (and denied) inner weakness. We cannot come together and be equals—we have too much to hide. At

home father was the top dog. The top dog had the power.
The rest of us had to do what he said. We have never
seen much equality in our lives, and it is hard to value it.
We *have* seen competition, and we have seen the rewards
that come to those who succeed. We want to be like
them.

It somehow didn't occur to any of us to look behind the
power. Who was father behind his bluster and demands?
Chances are he was a little person pretending to be a big
person. It was his secret, and it drove him to excess. He
claimed knowledge he didn't have. He claimed morality
he didn't have. Why did he need to be in charge and be
right?

VII

The sentimental history of America found in high
school history books is shorn of much that is not favor-
able. Accounts of the White Man's butchery and swindle
of the Native Americans are but brief overviews. The
enduring pain of Black people condemned to live in slavery, ghettos, prisons, and to feel the brunt of White exploitation is not presented in depth. Poor Americans,
from overworked textile workers, poorly paid farm workers, millions of people in minimum wage jobs, those
handicapped, maimed, illiterate, addicted, mentally ill, or
hobbled in some other way are not represented.

The accounts do not mention the legions of people who
are heart-broken, caught in meaningless jobs with mean-

ingless futures, so lonely they are out of their minds, or too broke to buy a newspaper.

The history of America is painted with an up-beat brush. The American Portrait Gallery in Washington, D.C. is filled with portraits of wealthy people, mostly male and White, whose reason for inclusion has to be explained to us—we don't know them. Women are but ghosts in the hallways.

The account of wholesome, White America is as common as, say, apple pie. It is a reassuring fantasy of a land beautiful beyond measure where everyone has a chance at the American dream and where virtue is rewarded with riches. It sounds as wonderful as it is idiotic.

The most important culture or frame for any of us is the culture or frame we have in our mind. We each live in a world we think. The apple pie vision of American excludes most of the things I have been describing, and it is for that reason it is a deflection. It is a vision that is not real.

Since it is important for us to feel good about the country in which we live, the presented view is positive. The culture, however, is split into numerous sub-sets. Each of these sub-sets must garner positive feelings in order to flourish. The problem is that the sub-sets collide with each other.

Democrats or Republicans are held to be either good or bad. This holds for all other categories: White or Black, rich or poor, religious or non-religious, male or female, educated or not educated, East Coast or West Coast, city dwellers or rural people, employed or not employed, &c.

In this sense there are many cultures that make up the whole. We are not a monolith; we are a plurality. In order to survive and be strong we need to find a way to get along with each other. Yet, all too often, that is not the culture we have.

We have a culture in which one sub-set is polarized and pitted against another. The haves seek to retain their advantage over the have nots. That this arrangement also harms the haves remains largely unseen. Soon we are not living in the wider culture; we are living in our own groups. And our group is defined in opposition to other groups.

Such arrangements come to us as by a birthright. We are born into groups (frames), and we learn to operate within them. While some attempt to transcend their original groups, others seek to defend them against all others. Besides there is an economic factor involved. One does not want to give up the economic advantage of one's group.

Sometimes to maintain one's group, one must become blind and deaf to the suffering all about one. One must not think about people in the city who don't have enough to eat. One must not think about people who are incarcerated due, not to justice but, to bigotry and ignorance. One must not think about people dying without adequate medical care. One must not think of people crushed under impossible debt. The list continues.

Our parents were college graduates, so we are. Our parents had good jobs, so we do. Our parents were healthy, so we are. Of course we had to work, but we had a chance to work. We were admitted, hired, treated. We would not like to think about giving these things up.

At issue is what sort of culture we have in our minds. Is it a culture that is attempting to be inclusive—with some sort of shared identity—or is it not? Are we angry with others or one with them? Are we, as Stephan Zweig suggested, not citizens of a country, but citizens of the world? What exactly do we call home?

If we are only interested in culture in so far as it pertains to us, we are functioning narcissistically. We are only thinking of ourselves. We vote for what is good for us but not good for others. "No one cares about me, so why should I care about anyone else?" The focus is not on the culture but on myself. It is about me.

VIII

Reflective function is the capacity to think about others as having thoughts and feelings of their own the same way I have thoughts and feelings of my own (Fonagy, 2001). As a result of this my own thoughts and feelings are seen as resonating with another's thoughts and feelings. This leads to an interpersonal connection and a capacity for empathy.

Such a process is important, because it is essential how a mother holds her infant in her mind. Though the infant has yet to develop organized thought, being regarded as if he or she is a wonderful creature of worth with important feelings renders him or her human. When reflective function is present and reliable, the infant is able to develop a secure attachment. He or she is known and acknowledged. This will be his or her basis for interactions in the world.

The infant's attachment pattern is a piece of implicit procedural memory that comprises the infant's unthought discovered way of interacting with another. With the subsequent development of language capacity, the child is also able to develop explicit memory concerning him or herself as well as others and patterns of relating. This capacity in turn allows for the development of identity and increased affect regulation.

In learning about the world the child responds to both elements in the world and also how the caregiver feels about them. In this way the child's response to an object comes to carry an emotional load. The child learns objects in the world matter the way his or her caregiver thinks they do.

When there are substantial breaches in reflective function the effect on the infant is that of being abandoned. In this situation the infant's sense of security and well-being is threatened. This in turn leads to thoughts of not being okay and may also lead to thoughts of being unlovable. An unlovable child is one that has something wrong with him or her. An unlovable child is unworthy.

Being not okay is to be inadequate. It is to feel unworthy of love and inclusion. It is to feel less than others. Inner feelings of being inadequate and unlovable will color subsequent interpretations of events. If I feel no one cares about what I think or feel at home, I will feel I don't matter in the world. This requires me to find a way to matter.

One way I can compensate for deep feelings of inadequacy is to appear strong and capable. That is, the feelings of inadequacy may be concealed behind a capable facade. It is important to be capable in the world, so if I appear as capable, no one will know the truth. I can have this thought, because I have grown up in a family in which real or actual thoughts and feelings are not considered or are carefully hidden.

This development is what Winnicott (1992) called the *false self*. The false self hides the real self and is more acceptable in the child's context.

It seems to work. If I appear strong and capable, others seem to take me that way. My secret is safe. But every time I fail to succeed at something, my real feelings are kicked up—and I feel inadequate again. This is painful, so I seek to avoid such instances. Instead I stick with those who buy my performance and think I am capable.

I avoid people who don't buy my performance. I devalue them, so I don't have to notice I fear them. I need them to play my game and see me as special. Depending on the relationship between us, I may ignore them, or seek to destroy them.

The result is a constructed world of the appearance of worth alongside the real world—in which I secretly feel unworthy. I try to live as much as possible in the constructed world where I feel I have value. I develop a facade to cover my (I feel) defective reality.

This is the development of narcissistic structure. It develops from a lack of reflective function. My mother may lose reflective function when she is overwhelmed in some fashion. If my mother is herself narcissistic, I either have a facade-mother, or I have a mother that is constantly losing focus due to being overwhelmed. The self-esteem of such a mother is always in flux.

If there is sufficient threat, any individual or group may lose reflective function and respond to the threatening other or group in a non-human way—as a bad object. This effect can be noticed even in individuals who are otherwise normally empathic. The loss of reflective function can lead to a lack of ownership of one's behavior, as though the behavior simply came out of nowhere (e.g. crowd hysteria). Such effects, for example, have been noted in response to great atrocities.

Narcissistic vulnerability stems from feelings of being ashamed about who I am. This can exist even though my parents and others say they love me and lavish all kinds of attention on me. A deep sense of not being seen or heard may have led to feelings of being essentially unlovable. If the attunement one has experienced is flawed or inadequate, one will feel alone. A child who feels alone is a child who will find it hard to feel loved.

Rage, resentment, and polarization in a society may be seen as ways to manage deep-seated feelings of inadequacy and worthlessness which stem from being unheard. The anger exhibited toward another group takes place in the absence of reflective function concerning that other group. Its members are conceived of in inhuman terms.

The more another group is attacked and devalued the greater the probability is that the other group will respond by attacking and devaluing in turn. It becomes a self-sustaining circle. Here the stated issue may not be the important part. Protecting against feelings of inadequacy and worthlessness may be the ultimate motivation.

When the basic focus of a society is competition over wealth and power, reflective function suffers. Soon everyone is competing against everyone else. There is no space in such an environment for resonance with another person's thoughts and feelings—both those with whom one agrees as well as those with whom one disagrees. No one is heard. A profound sort of psychological isolation occurs.

IX

Hope is an essential component of motivation. I will keep working if I have hope my work will lead to something worthwhile. When I have no hope my efforts will ever amount to anything, motivation falls apart.

In order to have hope I need to believe I may matter. I have to believe I can become more healthy, more knowledgeable, more valuable, and that I can become a more significant presence in the lives of other people.

Hope may be stifled in many different ways. I may be stuck in an essentially meaningless job, a stagnant relationship, a joyless routine, or a devaluing situation I cannot find a way to transcend. It is not only the poor who may be stuck. I may live an essentially meaningless life behind my wealth or success.

A rewarding life requires meaningful experiences with other people—either in fact or in my mind. It is in this interpersonal exchange I find welcome and understanding. It is here I am known. The more I am able to know and resonate with another, the more meaningful the interaction becomes.

When my experiences with others have been unrewarding or traumatic I am left without a place to share my thoughts and feelings. This leaves me in the position of being unknown. And if I am unknown the risk rises I will feel unacceptable.

If I was raised in a home in which people didn't welcome my thoughts and feelings, a home in which only behavior mattered, I may have been taught only my father's or my mother's feelings mattered. They had the power, and they determined how things went. I learned only those who have power matter.

When one has no hope and doesn't matter, one's life is filled with emptiness. A nation filled with such people cannot be strong or consider itself humane. When the haves and have-nots lose mobility, hope is lost.

The solution—if one is possible—is always incremental. It is always wise to find a place where there is some hope. Hope stems from being heard. From mattering. A healthy culture attempts to find ways to help people to matter. It does this by regarding them as worthy of being heard. A culture that doesn't listen to its people is inhumane and toxic.

X

It is easy to say the answer is that we need to resonate with and include more people. It is, however, something else to go about doing just that.

The truth is we don't have enough collective self-esteem to accomplish such a thing. This is the case as the response we constantly encounter in public is a lack of caring or even hostility. We are set up to ignore or move against each other, and it will not be easy to make any dent in that.

Anger and hopelessness come about from damage to the self. Healing a damaged self is a significant undertaking.

Not being inert and hostile in public is possible. The more people who respond to others in an open way, the better every day is.

The American experiment has discovered that a humane society cannot operate without humanity. Unbridled entitlement and greed are not characteristics of healthy psychologies, and polarization and hate quickly become destructive. We have landed at the last stop on the train line.

The struggle for power is dangerous in a culture of self-focus. This is true as self-focus is a result of bitter childhood frustration. Our attempt to have parents assume the role of authorities has failed. Children don't need authorities as much as they need empathic understanding. Abusive parenting leads to crippled children—and adults.

Each one who tries to grasp how it must feel to be another person contributes to the solution. It is often the case that for someone to win, another must lose. Horney (1994) spoke of the great American wish to be first and foremost in all things and simultaneously loved by all. When such a wish is stripped of care for others, it leads to disaster. Achievement alone is not enough. Amassing wealth is not enough. To be healthy a psychology must experience a profound attachment to other psychologies.

The American society today has resulted in categories of inhumanity. One such category includes managers and directors of business. By focusing on profit alone, what is human has been cut out of these endeavors. When workers are reduced to ciphers and hourly units of production, anything beyond profit loses value. The result is ever more shoddy widgets at cheaper and cheaper prices. Also, when widgets become the only markers of value, items are amassed in a frantic attempt to matter. Soon, it becomes a society of widgets instead of a society of people—that is, the widgets matter more than the people. We don't want Frank. We want his Mercedes.

The mismatch between the financial situation of those who make the widgets and those who order such widgets grows wider. The widget makers can afford less and less while the widget managers and directors make more and more. Soon whole areas of life are beyond the reach of the widget makers. Good schools, quality medical care, opportunities to grow and develop slip farther and farther out of reach.

At the same time, dissevered from meaningful contact with the culture in which they live, managers and directors seclude themselves from the workers and occupy themselves with their own possessions. This robs them of meaningful human exchange on any substantial scale and leads to a distortion of values. A point is reached when contact between managers and workers is all but non-existent. They, importantly, do not share the same culture.

Of course human exploitation is not a new phenomenon, and it has always threatened to tear cultures apart. But if we take on the task of building a humane and just society, this is a gap that must find a solution. Further that solution must be an inclusive rather than an exclusive arrangement. Even children know the rules of fairness—unless some bully beats it out of them.

A good manager, as a good parent, is concerned that those under his or her guidance are flourishing. When this is the focus, the operation is allowed to function optimally. Yet, such a strategy shifts the focus away from profit-above-all. A maximally functioning operation that stresses psychological health is the tide that lifts all boats.

This means everyone's feelings get to matter. It requires that each person feels he or she can be heard and genuinely considered. Healthy families operate this way and so do healthy operations.

It is precisely this outcome that is sacrificed when the only consideration is maximizing profit. And when the profit generated benefits an extreme minority alone, the operation has become inhumane pure and simple. This is what has happened in the last twenty or so years in America. The drive for profit alone shuttered whole sectors of American production—without considering how to manage the immense psycho-social fallout that would ensue. In fact there was little concern from any sector about the fallout that would occur. The result was what Case and Deaton (2020) called "deaths of despair."

The result was a society that did not work for those without a college degree. Incredibly, this was a majority of the working age population (Gawande, 2020). The way in which American society has dealt with long-term economic stagnation has left White men without a college degree to search for the only work available to them. This includes unstable employment with uncertain hours, jobs shorter in duration, gig work, temporary contracting, and day-labor. Such employment notoriously lacks bene-fits including health insurance.   The health insurance problem is greater than it appears due to its expense, both to consumer and employer, its difficulty of access, and its inadequate coverage. For workers earning half the medi-an wage, health care expenses can be sixty percent of their income (Ibid.).

Those at the bottom of the earnings scale are often ig-nored or devalued by the society that values wealth and power. Gawande (Ibid) wrote:

> When it comes to people whose lives aren't going well, American culture is a harsh judge. If you can't find enough work, if your wages are too low, if you can't be counted on to support a family, if you don't have a promising future, then there must be something wrong with you…We Americans are reluctant to acknowledge that our econ-omy serves the educated classes and penal-izes the rest.

The challenge for the business and political communi-ties is how to humanely address the problems of poverty and valuelessness. If we are to strive for optimal mental health, we must find a way for more people to have digni-ty. The increasing gap between the haves and the have-nots must narrow.

Such comments are especially relevant to the way in which health care has been managed in this country, that is in the service of profits for corporations. It is by no means clear that health care can be simultaneously focused on quality and on profit. The way this has typically be attempted is definitionally. The American system of health care has long been the world's most complicated and expensive, but it does not deliver the best results. It is a matter of purpose. Optimal results must be prioritized over optimal profits.

It is clearly the case that increased education results in viewpoints markedly different from those found with less education. This is more than a gulf between those who prefer Mozart to country music, it is a growing respect for the academic work involved in significant undertakings such as science, arts, developed sophistication, historical understanding, and improved living conditions.

While it is true animosity is easy to find among the lesser educated for the more educated, it remains also true that the animosity can run the other way as well. Just as the business group has its snobs, so does the academic group. As the culture develops, the gap between these groups widens in similar ways to which it widens in terms of wealth. Soon, there is little to no communication between groups.

It must be said that snobbishness is not an inevitable result of education. In fact, it may be evidence against it. The need to appear superior to others reveals poor ego strength in both the educated and the wealthy. There is no reason Don Giovanni cannot be staged in the same city as The Country Music Review. These are different tastes akin to different tastes in food or exercise. Different is not the same as opposition.

Part of being fortunate enough to be able to pursue greater education is a requirement to use that education to benefit others in addition to oneself. Educated people are a tremendous asset to any culture unless they squander that education on self-focus and self-aggrandizement. Again, in order to have a culture in which it is worthwhile to live, there must be an option to the policy of everyone for him or herself. This is not an outrageous requirement. Doing something to give back each day shifts one's balance.

Many religions came to the modern era with a list of demands governing how people should behave. Often these were issued by autocratic leaders and allowed for little deviance. There is, however, a mismatch between autocratic directives and nurturing support.

Psychological science has tended to undermine authority as a basis for thinking and behaving. The importance of empathy in mother-child bonding is profound in determining the future mental health of the infant (see Aikin, 2020). This requires much more than proper behavior or attending to the child's physical needs. Without an empathic attunement with another person, children miss a profound experience of being a human being who matters among other human beings who matter.

Religions have often battled one another in ways similar to the ways in which high school athletic teams battle one another. Lines have hardened. In this, the focus of religion has been lost. Over time it has become what I can get instead of what I can give. The focus is on compliance and strength instead of mercy. Such approaches have contributed to distance and polarization instead of unity and interpersonal concern.

Failures of American culture to empathically treat Black people have resulted in a major disgrace in addition to racial injustice. Built on the backs of Native and enslaved people, the American system has routinely sought to relegate these people to inferior status. Much of this relegation has been accomplished by perfectly legal means. The prosperity of one group required the poverty of the other. Whether huddled onto reservations or into ghettos, powerful legal and economic regulations perpetuate injustice. And entire segments of the society simply look the other way.

It is clear White males have always been the ascendant group in this country. The whole tapestry of social structure is designed to perpetuate that category as supreme. There is simply too much profit in keeping it that way. Besides, *they* are not *us*. We have our hands full worrying about ourselves.

Each of these categories of inhumanity exist due to emphasis on greed and self-focus to the exclusion of empathy and compassion. America, the land of the rugged individualists, has become a land of competing strangers. Whether greed is founded on wealth, educational status, or ideology, it is a principle that is self-destructive. Just as the English commons was destroyed by selfishness, so any culture in which people have no concern for one another becomes fragmented.   And like the destruction of the commons, if everyone is struggling to get as much as he or she can, there are inevitably those who are left with nothing.   These people either have to be cared about or ignored.

Increasingly in American culture we have chosen to ignore them. No society can be great that sacrifices a significant proportion of its inhabitants on the altar of greed. This is especially true since not all inhabitants are able to line up at the same starting line or even remotely close to the same starting line.

Based on the theory that if two aspirins are good, twenty-two must be better, our culture has allowed healthy striving and various forms of power to get out of hand. Some single families have amassed enough wealth to end childhood hunger in our country. Whether or not this is a concern swings on whose child is hungry. A readjustment must begin somewhere.

It begins with each person. As in psychotherapy an awareness of the problem allows for helpful action. Once I realize uninhibited greed and self-focus is destructive, I can monitor these impulses in myself. I must do this as, being part of this culture, such impulses have come to me in the very air I breathe. I am the one who has to think about what I am giving as well as what I am getting.

Each of us who tries to find a value beyond money and power must find a way to pass this reorientation on. When a society becomes good for a select few and bad

for everybody else that society may be described as toxic.
It is not a good place to live. It needs our help.

XI

It is important to consider the issue of psychopathic
people. A good deal of police brutality has been justified
in terms of the necessity to deal with psychopaths. The
problem has been that all people tend to be treated with
brutality instead of reserving strict and forceful boundaries for psychopaths alone.

Persons with psychopathic personalities are those who
have been severely damaged in their childhoods, often by
the brutality that is used to constrain them. Though there
is evidence of genetic involvement in psychopathic development (Gabbard, 2014), people who become psychopaths routinely come from homes in which they were
not treated in humane ways. Their feelings were irrelevant. Their needs were ignored. They were often treated
with violence, and the logic of their environments seemed
to indicate that in all things, you either win or you lose.

Such backgrounds lacked empathy as empathy was
seen as a trap, a weakness. If everyone is out to get
everyone else, it is better to be impervious and appear
"strong." Psychopathic individuals move against others
before those others can move against them. They are famous for lacking remorse. Illegal acts are common as is
a pervasive lack of trust.

White-collar psychopaths are typically less violent than their lower-class counterparts. Their field of activity routinely involves manipulations of money, work-place interactions, and politics.

Most forms of psychotherapy are ineffective in treating psychopaths. A rigidly controlled environment manned by incorruptible personnel produces the best results (Gabbard, Ibid).

This highly crime-prone group has elicited a developed police response. Psychopaths are hard to manage. Restraints against bad behavior that are effective with other people (e.g., laws) don't work with psychopaths. Conflict is almost always involved.

Obviously, narcissism is involved in psychopathy. The psychopathic person is the one who matters. Other people do not matter. Maximizing the returns to the self as well as screwing other people over is a routine pattern. Such individuals are a disaster in organizations, families, and politics.

It is clear these people are deviant. They are badly damaged in ways they may never overcome. Still, it is the case a truly humane society must attempt to treat them in the most appropriate ways. Simply having the police battle them and throw them in jail, without any attempt to rehabilitate them, solves little.

A cultural shift is required. Psychopaths are the products of extremely unhealthy childhoods. They have often been treated sadistically. In such cases, the problem is the parents. It is the parents who require treatment. And this is why one-size-fits-all treatment programs are destined to fail. Not all parents are problematic. The place to intervene is in the childhood and with the parents of problem children. This shifts the emphasis from police use of force to helpful interventions.

If such childhood interventions are not prioritized, children from harmful homes will grow into difficult to manage adults. The wound will not have been treated when the treatment could help. It will have to be treated with brutality similar to that which created it in the first place.

It is known that secure attachment results in children who feel safe and welcome. These children tend to be empathically connected to others and to live humane lives. The institutions of society are comprised of people. If these people are empathically attuned they operate much differently than do people who lack empathy. The difference is between talking *with* someone versus talking *at* someone.

The same holds for parents and for police departments. Many parents and police persons are trained to seize *control* of the situation and to proceed in an autocratic fashion. This is an approach designed for managing psychopaths and few others. How different it would be if the approach were to help people work out their issues and get along. In this case parents and police would approximate the role of nurturing parents instead of demanding ones. It is a shift in tone toward a more humane outcome.

XII

America has certainly had its troubles in trying to grow and develop. It has focused much of its energy on developing wealth and power. These two routinely run together in such a way that the goal is the power of wealth. Attaining this is the impetus behind widespread effort.

Far less emphasis has been placed on emotional well-being. The result is that our society is better at dealing with power than it is dealing with emotional well-being. In some circles dealing with emotional well-being is irrelevant. A heavy price has been paid for this approach.

In the sixties there was considerable debate concerning a war in Viet Nam. The "establishment" (the power) wanted to proceed and defeat the "enemy." Young people, who were supposed to do the fighting, balked. They could not see the sense in fighting and dying for something in which they did not believe. The establishment reacted poorly—with force. This led to nation-wide, escalating confrontations in which the goal was not understanding but crushing of the opposition.

Parents were pitted against their children. The society split into those who supported the establishment and its power and those who reacted against it. Bill Clinton is reported to have said, "If you thought the Sixties were a good thing, you are probably a Democrat. If you thought the Sixties were a bad thing, you are probably a Republican."

This split has only grown wider in the Trump era.

Clearly, development implies an embrace of what is new. This is very frightening to some people. They grew up in homes that did not embrace what was new. Father ruled with an iron hand. His word was law. New things simply threatened that and were rejected out of hand. If my family was one in which people's feelings got to count, listening to new things was routine.

The result is a group of citizens poor in the art of growing. The violence with which America essentially stole the land from Native Americans, the violence with which they heartlessly enslaved an entire group of African people, the violence with which affairs were conducted in the Old West—all have taken their toll.

Today Black people are widely subject to police brutality, businesspeople routinely cheat and steal at a significant level, and politicians have split into groups in order to battle and try to defeat each other.

Authoritarianism has a solid place in our culture. Backed by power and lacking empathy, it permeates school systems, police systems, court systems, business systems, political systems, and families. It demands its dictates are followed and punishes noncompliance. It has destroyed relationships, fractured generations, ruined lives, and created an inhospitable environment.

The upshot is there is no place where children can be treated in caring and humane ways and learn what it is like to be part of an empathic environment. Many feel no hope. Aliens at home, in school, at church and ordered around everywhere, it is hard to buy into the collective. Even the God they imagine is punitive.

Psychology, the science of the human par excellence, is itself riddled with autocrats who teach non-empathic methods of treatment. Experiments are severely restricted to worn out empirical frameworks that are poor at dealing believably with emotions and pain.

Still, psychology offers an option to rigid authoritarianism. Done properly it offers listening, empathy, the chance to work through and resolve childhood trauma, and the development of an effective working self. This is a role society would do well to cultivate.

For many people, the first time they experience an intimate, empathic, and caring relationship is in psychotherapy. It is this environment as much as the working through of negative influences from one's past that makes the impact so profound.

It is not as if there is a choice. Either we learn how to consider and include each other, or we will destroy each other. And for what? To protect the weakness of those who must have power over others? This is not a phenomenon worth protecting. Weakness, skin color, and limited means need not be a problem. The problem is inhumanity.

REFERENCES

Aikin, P. A. Privation: Winnicott's Forgotten Concept: Application to Contemporary Psychoanalytic Treatment. Academia, 2020.

Case, A. and Deaton, A. Deaths of Despair and the Future of Capitalism. Princeton, 2020.

Coutu, D. I Was Greedy, Too. Harvard Business Review, 02-2003.

Fairbairn, W.R.D. Psychoanalytic Studies of the Personality. Routledge, 1994.

Fonagy, P. Attachment Theory and Psychoanalysis. Other, 2001.

Foucault, M. The Order of Things: An Archeology of the Human Sciences. Random House, 1970.

Gabbard, G.O. Psychodynamic Psychiatry in Clinical Practice. Fifth Edition. American Psychiatric Press, 2014.

Gadamer, H-G. Truth and Method. Crossroad, 1989.

Gallo, A. How the American Dream Turned into Greed and Inequality. World Economic Forum, 09-11-2017.

Gwande, A. The Blight: How our Economy Created an Epidemic of Despair. New Yorker, 03-23-2020.

Heidegger, M. Existence and Being. Gateway, 1949.

Hinshelwood, R.D., and Fortuna, T. Melanie Klein (The Basics). Routledge, 2017.

Horney, K. The Neurotic Personality of our Time. Norton, 1994.

Jones, E. The Life and Work of Sigmund Freud. Basic, 1961.

Kahloon, I. The Leveler: Tomas Piketty Goes Global in "Capital and Ideology." New Yorker, 03-09-2020.

Kohut, H. How Does Analysis Cure? Chicago, 1984.

Lakoff, G. The Political Mind: A Cognitive Scientist's Guide to Your Brain and its Politics. Penguin. 2009.

Lakoff, G. Moral Politics: How Liberals and Conservatives Think. Third Edition. Chicago, 2016.

Lakoff, G. Understanding Trump. RSN, 08-15-16.

Leonhardt, D. Dying of 'Despair' in America. New York Times, 03-08-2020.

Lind, M. The New Class War: Saving Democracy from the Managerial Elite. Portfolio/Penguin, 2020.

Lyotard, J-F., The Postmodern Condition: A Report on Knowledge. Minnesota, 1984.

Mann, B. The Toxic Masculinity of the Trump Administration. New York Times, 10-21-19.

Mann, B. Sovereign Masculinity: Gender Lessons from the War on Terror. Oxford University Press, 2014.

Piketty, T. Capital in the Twenty-First Century. Belknap Press, 2014.

Piketty, T. Capital and Ideology. Harvard. 2020.

Riviera, E. P. The Linked Self in Psychoanalysis. (Eds.) R. Losso, L.S. DeSetton, and D. Sharff. Routledge, 2017.

Winnicott, D. W. Through Pediatrics to Psycho Analysis: Collected Papers. Brunner/Mazel, 1992.

PANDEMIC

The pandemic caused by the coronavirus hit the United States at exactly the wrong time. Caught in a political backlash to the Obama years, the government was engaged in a process of tearing down what had been built before. Under the Trump administration, agencies were gutted, experienced personal were lost, money was reallocated from health organizations to defense, and the health care system, riddled by corporate greed and overcontrol, was functioning poorly for those of limited means. In short, there was an attempt to rid government of people with intelligence.

If the Obama years were the time of the bright kids in class, the Trump years were the time of the toughs and bullies. These toughs and bullies sought to cover up any weakness they had with the appearance of strength and bravado. This was how they thought about things and how they acted.

The appearance of strength, however, was no match for the coronavirus. The virus was something that required both a scientific and medical solution, not a fist-fight. The bullies and toughs were impotent in the face of the illness and left to bluster and threaten.

Thus the virus, in addition to killing hundreds of thousands of people, focused a clear light on a sizable portion of the population that was maladaptive and angry. Further, this was anger that had few avenues for expression. No match for any enterprise that required adaptive intelligence, the bullies were forced to see their only asset was brute strength and a capacity for labor—training that enabled compliance with power.

The solution to bullies and toughs is not more power. It is finding intelligent and workable solutions. Psychology is the science that has sought to understand bullies and toughs. Where do they come from? How are they created?

Though all cultures reflect a naturally occurring difference in intellectual ability, it may be seen that differences in intellectual ability alone do not account for the development of bullies and toughs.

Hurt is required.

Ordinary human development includes training in strategies for managing anger. Anger, the emotion itself, is not the problem. The problem is what to *do* with it. There are many things that can be done with anger, for example:

> Yelling and screaming
> Hitting things and people
> Breaking things
> Stuffing it
> Converting it into its opposite: kindness (re-action formation)
> Delinquent acts
> Walking it off
> Becoming passive-aggressive
> Becoming oppositional

This list could be extended. But there is also another thing that can be done with anger: *talking about it.* In fact, this option is often superior to others. If things can be talked about, solutions can often be found. It is when anger cannot be talked about that significant problems arise.

The process of psychotherapy routinely explores the ways in which one was parented as a child. If my parents could hear my anger toward them, tried to understand it, and helped me to understand it as well, I likely grew up with a healthy ability to deal with anger and other strong emotions.

If, on the other hand, my parents could not tolerate expressions of my anger toward them, I was forced to find other ways to manage my anger (see the list above). In this case, anger becomes much more than one of the emotions one feels in life and becomes instead something dangerous. Anger may directly lead to pain and anguish.

Additionally, my parents were either angry people or they were not. They lived lives of struggle or they did not. They got on well with others or they did not. They were able to be genuinely pleasant with me or they were not. I knew their innermost thoughts, or I did not, &c.

The way my parents dealt with their emotions contributed a great deal to the world they constructed in my childhood home. It was a safe place to be or it was not. It was stable or it was not. Differing options were welcomed or they were not.

In short, the emotional "climate" of my childhood home was the climate to which I learned to adapt and to which my developing neurons wired. It became my "normal" (see Riviere, 2017, Gabbard, 2014). This is a semi-complex way to underline the fact we have not had the same, sometimes even similar, experiences in life. In terms of effective contexts our psychologies have experienced, we have lived in different worlds.

This is a fact our society has not directly addressed. We are thought to be a giant melting-pot where every difference is accepted and welcomed. This, in fact, has never been true. In order for us to be an accepting and welcoming melting-pot, we all have to matter in some sense. This is where the rub comes in.

Self-esteem requires that we feel welcome and of value. In many of our backgrounds, we were neither welcome nor of value. In fact, no one had any value, and no one was really welcome. Many of us were a burden at best, and our parents did not treat us as people who had thoughts and feelings just as they had. We were, in short, *objects*. Everyone was seen as an object, and the only worth about objects was the power or the money they had.

Our parents may have thought money was the only thing that matters. They may have thought this about academic achievement. It may have been sports prowess or physical strength. And, since like-people tend to find each other, it is possible everyone we knew in our neighborhood or in our parents' circles were similar.

We thought: Everyone thinks this way.

But they don't. We had only met the people who lived in our town, who were of our religion, race, cultural level, or SES. It is likely our experience is of a group. And it is also likely the group reflects the same understandings back to us that support the group. This forms the backbone of what is known as "local culture."

It is the group, therefore, that determines one's worth. We will be rated in terms of how we fit into what the group values. This may work either for or against any one person. The hierarchy of value is established by the group, or the family, and this is considered to be how the world *is*, or how the world *should* be. It is the template for how people are to behave.

What is missed in such a process is that it is only the group (or the family, the region, those similar) that feels this way. Academic ability might mean little where I am from. Treating people with understanding might indicate some giant training-failure.

As children were are sent to school. This is a kind of amalgamation but only to an extent. It is likely my peers come from families similar to my own. They live in the same area. Their parents do similar kinds of work and make similar kinds of money. I may get to know several different kinds of personalities, but cultural messages about how the world is, and people are, may be quite the same.

In this way our lives become stratified into groups with similar experiences and outlooks and separate from groups with dissimilar experiences and outlooks.

The problem is that these groups are not similarly valued.

Deprived of worth by being ignored— or worse, ridiculed—some group will seek to rise in power. Bereft of empathy, this group will assume that power over others is a virtue. An ideal way to attain power over others is to *devalue* them, treat them as worthless or inferior—and refuse to allow them to rise in stature.

Controlling the valuation system bestows immense power. This is especially true if one has the ear of those one seeks to devalue. Power in this sense consists in having an opinion that matters.

People will go to considerable lengths to keep from feeling worthless. In this way, self-worth is able to become a significant motivator. We are drawn to what values us, and we avoid what finds us of no value. This creates a fertile climate for sub-groups. In school we find our groups. We are drawn to them and drawn away from others. We like to be where we are accepted, and we feel uncomfortable where we are not.

The troublemakers have no desire to find themselves amid the good kids and vice versa. Such divisions may be seen in terms of different sensibilities. These may also include income and educational levels, as well differences between working class and professional or upper-class groups. These groups may experience widely different kinds of lives, in different kinds of places.

Differences between groups are to be expected and are ordinary. Differences themselves are not the problem. The problem has to do with how different groups treat each other. When different groups seek to welcome and include each other, plurality and harmony results. It is when groups compete with or attack each other that larger social issues arise.

The anger and the attack is routinely bi-directional. That is, the groups involved oppose each other. Such opposition may be overt or concealed, verbal or physical, as well as legal or illegal (see Coates, 2015).

We do not routinely attack or oppose people who like us, welcome us, and value us. We attack or oppose people who don't do these things. This is how the "good kids" are not as blameless as they appear. The good kids typically have a negative view of the bad kids. Opportunities are not extended, friendship offered, &c. The bad kids treat the good kids the same way.

In fact, one way to understand groups the most is to learn who or what the group *opposes*. You will never belong to a group if you don't oppose who or what the group opposes.

Soon groups are polarized.

When they become polarized, they tend to operate in separate circles and have little contact—except at conflict points. The good kids get jobs and keep the bad kids from getting jobs, for example. The good kids set the bad kids up for aggressive acts and then protest innocence when the bad kids get in trouble. Soon, the entire school, from the faculty on down, are complicit in this charade. It is a rigged game. The good kids prevail, and the bad kids take the rap.

The result of this game is anger. This anger grows and is focused on whatever is considered opposition. Over time, the good kids do better and better while the bad kids do worse and worse. Soon they are living in different parts of town, if they are not there already, doing different kinds of work, and responding to increasingly different sub-cultures.

The anger doesn't go away. This is the case as the larger culture assigns positive labels to the good kids and negative labels to the bad kids. The good kids have the nice houses in the nice places, and their kids are going to the nice schools. The bad kids are relegated elsewhere.

Of course, this description is a cartoon. Families, like groups, are not monolithic. It is nevertheless the case that our culture tends to value people according to the groups they represent. The approved groups *do* look down their noses at the non-approved groups. This *does* give rise to rage. Soon, everybody hates everybody, and the sense of a common culture comes apart.

Anger tends to beget anger.

Belonging to a group may become part of one's identity. When this is the case, one tends to obtain his or her sense of worth from group participation. That is, the group is like-minded and therefore approving of one's membership in it. Members of the in-group are valued, whereas members of the out-group are devalued. This makes the idea of leaving the group very difficult.

We are born into families that are associated with some groups and not with others. Our parents obtain some of their worth from the groups in which they feel they belong. As children, our behavior, if not our being, is valued by our parents and the groups to which they belong. If the working-class group to which we belong hates rich people, we learn this mode of behavior. If the upper-class group to which we belong avoids interactions with working-class people, we learn this mode of behavior.

The process of polarization can go too far. Polarized groups can threaten the existence of the whole. This results in a kind of warfare of attitudes if not efforts. Such a split occurs when the sub-group is seen by its members as more important that the maintenance of the whole. The sub-group, for example, may consider itself to be the "true" expression of the spirit of the whole. It may consider others to be a danger to the whole. (We are the true patriots.) In such a situation, feelings may become intense.

Some groups deliberately seek polarization as a component of their identity. They exist in order to break apart an intact whole. Examples of this situation abound.

The obvious question is: Why are so many people spending so much time and going to such lengths to receive some recognition of their worth? Or, in other words, why do so many people feel their worth is in question? Why is acknowledgement of worth in such short supply?

It is easy to see not all children are treated as persons of worth in their homes. Achievement may be valued or compliance, but where are the acknowledgements of worth—of being of worth simply because you are a person?

Lakoff (2009, 2016) argued there are strict-father families and nurturing-parent families. In the strict-father family, father is considered to be the head authority, and everyone is to comply with what the father says. Children are to behave, whatever that is in a particular family. When they do not behave, they are punished severely enough that they will not mis-behave in the future. Compliance with the father's word is the goal.

In nurturing-parent families, on the other hand, the child is helped to discover his or her identity—and how to be that person. Here, the child is helped to stand on his or her own feet and interact with the world according to his or her abilities. Thoughts and feelings of the child are heard and honored.

An example of an exchange in a nurturing-parent family might be the following.

"I hate you," says the child to his father.

"I see you are angry" says the father.

"What are you angry about?"

"You didn't let me play with Frank!" says the child.

"I see I didn't handle that very well, did I?" says the father.

"Here's what I was thinking: you have a paper to write for school on Monday. You have postponed doing it for two days. I don't blame you for postponing it, but it really has to be done. If you went with Frank, you would have no chance to get it done, and would have had to do a sloppy, rush job."

"I don't care!"

"Okay, how do you think I could have done this better?"

"Stop patrolling me" says the child.

"Okay, how would you like to get your work done, so that I don't have to say anything?"

And so on.

In this example, the child is heard, the parent does not act like an imperial paragon, the channels of communication are opened, and the child is given a chance to help construct a solution to the problem. That is to say, the focus is on a psychologically healthy solution to the problem. Had the father demanded blind compliance with his demand, he may have achieved this, but at what cost?

The cost would have been anger. All parties would likely have been angry, and this anger would not have helped solve the problem. It would have added hurt feelings to the relationship.

Experimental psychologists (see, for example, Meyers and Hansen, 2011; Terry, 2017; Martin and Pear, 2014; Rimm and Masters, 1974) long ago found punishment is a non-optimal means of controlling behavior. In the control of behavior, according to the paradigm of operant conditioning, there are three possible responses to an instance of behavior.

The behavior occurs and:

1. It may be rewarded.
2. It may be punished.
3. Nothing may happen.

If the behavior is rewarded, it will tend to occur again. If nothing happens, it likely will fade away. If punishment happens, chaos will result. Giving the dog a treat for fetching the ball will, all things being equal, result in the dog fetching the ball again when it is tossed. Doing nothing when the dog fetches the ball will, all things being equal, result in a diminishment in ball-fetching behavior (with no result, ball-fetching may initially increase, but if there is never any consequence to ball-fetching, it will tend to die out).

If the dog is punished for fetching the ball, chaotic results are likely to occur. Difficult to control emotional factors will be injected into the situation that will, in turn, be difficult to manage.

The point is that the creature will tend to behave in terms of the *consequences* of its behavior. The obvious conclusion is that if you want the creature to behave differently, you need to arrange the consequences differently. Wanting different behavior without changing anything will likely result in zero change.

But change does not *require* punishment. In fact, due to unavoidable emotional reactions, punishment may be a bad option. It certainly is not a *necessary* option.

There are, nevertheless, parents who seek to control their children by the use of punishment and fear. Here, the emphasis is on "proper" behavior (whatever this family considers that to be). The emphasis is not on empathic understanding.

There are millions of people who have been raised in a climate of punishment and fear. These people have not been heard and understood. They have, in short, been treated as objects. To them, this sort of treatment is experienced as ordinary. Unless some modification intervenes, they treat their own children the same way. They treat their employees the same way. They treat their students the same way. They offer no option.

What will the children of such people count as worth? Obedience and compliance? Resistance and rebellion? Will they drop out of the system and live as wounded survivors?

Clearly, the context in which such children were raised robbed them of a robust sense of worth for being who they are. They were taught their worth is contingent on something else (see Rogers, 1989). That is to say they are not simply worthwhile. They are only worthwhile *if* they have accomplished something. That something else is likely to be a form of compliance or achievement. It is not likely to be an attempt to find the worth in other people.

In this case human worth is, in itself, seen to be of lesser value than things like wealth, power, in-group affiliation, &c. One's position comes to take precedence over one's identity. Those things have worth. Being human plus a five-dollar bill will get you a cup of coffee.

The result is a society like the one we have in which human beings are far from being considered the most valued things—and certainly how they feel is not of great interest.

Polarity has always been a part of the American identity. We broke away from England, *those* people, and stole the land from the American Indians, *those* people. We imported slaves, *those* people, to till this land, and we enacted laws that kept us in the best circumstances and *those* people in the worst. It mattered where you belonged.

The problem of American racism is an example of White people setting themselves up as superior to Black people and institutionalizing this disparity into the culture (see next chapter).

The American Civil War pitted American against American as the very fabric of the society split apart. The two World Wars offered an easing to this split as national survival was at stake.

Then came the Sixties. As previously stated, the U.S. was involved in a hotly debated war in Indio-China where, as before, young people were sent to fight. Many young people did not see the purpose of fighting and dying for something they felt was wrong. Another split occurred.

Those in power, insisted the young people comply with their dictates and fight. Increasingly, young people began to refuse. This became its own war: the establishment against the war-protesters. Its authority challenged; the establishment reacted with force. Soon counter-force occurred. Malcolm X and Martin Luther King were assassinated as were the Kennedy brothers. Freedom Riders in the South were killed. Riots set cities aflame and students were killed at Kent State and at Jackson State. The Democratic Convention collapsed into violence with tanks patrolling the streets of Chicago (see Klein, 2020). Tanks!

Yet the 1960s were different. These were not *those* people. They were our own sons and daughters. We were turning on ourselves and destroying ourselves. It was our own neighborhoods on fire. This pitted parents against children and opened a wide divide.

The split was between those who demanded compliance and those who demanded the right to choose for themselves. Political parties were involved, Republicans largely supported compliance, whereas Democrats largely supported individual choice.

The American establishment has routinely sought to obtain and maintain dominion over those who do not support its unique claim to power. To assist it in this enterprise, it has developed its police forces to punish non-compliance. The result has been an ongoing campaign against *those* people and a benefiting of *our* people.

American business, with notable exceptions, operates on a compliance model. American politics runs this way as does the structure of American universities. Professions are licensed and require compliance. There is routinely a steep price to be paid for deviating from the system.

It is as if the strict-father is far more common than the nurturing-parent. Helping people develop and grow is often only supported when the development and growth is pointed in the "right" direction. In such a climate, humanity itself is the casualty.

During the time of the coronavirus, this system struggled and was badly exposed. Health care operations set up to benefit the establishment and the wealthy quickly became overwhelmed and were unable to meet the demand placed on them. There were over four million new infections. Between 100,000 and 200,000 Americans died, most of them elderly and people of color. Social distancing requirements left businesses unable to make a profit, and many failed. Millions of people were out of work.

Menon (2020) stated:

The novel SARS-CoV-2 has roared through the American landscape leaving physical, emotional, and economic devastation in its wake. By early July, known infections in this country exceeded three million, while deaths topped 135,000. Home to just over 4% of the global population, the United States accounts for more than a quarter of all fatalities from Covid-19, the disease produced by the coronavirus. Amid a recent surge of infections, especially across the Sun Belt, which Vice President Mike Pence typically denied was even occurring, the Centers for Disease Control and Prevention (CDC) reported that the daily total of infections had reached a record 60,000. Arizona's seven-day average alone approached that of the European Union, which has 60 times as many people.

Meanwhile the Trump administration was seen to have only one skill: attack. Devoid of empathy and unused to cooperation with anyone other than sympathetic rich people, the government could only be ineffective. It had no plan to manage the pandemic. All it had to offer was a vacuum.

That vacuum brought with it enormous mental health problems. Huge numbers of people were grieving the loss of loved ones. They were isolated due to requirements of social distancing. They had lost their income, or their income was seriously compromised. They had lost jobs, school opportunities, athletic placements, as well as access to restaurants, bars, churches, and other places of friendly gathering.

Whole lives were disrupted in significant ways, many for any foreseeable future. There was even a shortage of toilet paper.

The society was unable to deal with the mental health onslaught in the same way they were unable to deal with the pandemic. They had not yet devised a way to make money or otherwise benefit from it.   While myriads of people died due to the physical illness, many myriads more were left to suffer miserable lives. No one cared.

It is for the humans among us to think this whole thing through and try to generate improvements. What needs to be addressed is the culture's *psychology*. The strict-father is routinely not a healthy father. Autocratic heads of corporations and police departments are routinely not healthy people. In short, anyone who ignores what is human in favor of wealth, power, or position does us all a disservice and is in need of treatment. These are the people who built the rickety system in which we have been living.

A more humane society requires valuing what is human. Psychologically wounded people are the result of backgrounds that were emotionally or physically traumatic. No one listened to them—really listened. No one cared.

It is for us to gradually replace the strict-father leadership with a more nurturing one if we want a healthier society. This will be far from easy. Where it can begin is with awareness. Guns and force are not required. The consequences simply must be rearranged.

Concepts of mental health as well as the tragic consequences of physical and emotional trauma can be taught to students. Damaged students can be identified and helped. Businesses and corporations can pay attention to mental health issues in addition to profit and expansion. Police departments can be engaged in ongoing, daily interactions concerning mental health issues, both their own and others. We have to find a way to make life healthy in addition to our emphasis on wealth and power.

This is to say we must find a way to make mental health a value worth attaining. The system that supports people having obscene amounts of wealth while others are hungry is not contributing to general well-being. Quite the opposite. Valuing health and humanity may still be beyond the developmental level of the human race, but if it can take root somewhere, that somewhere is with children.

We must treat children better, nurture them more, inform them of health issues, and genuinely listen to what they have to say. These children will become parents, and the health and humanity of their children is at stake.

To accomplish this a radical reorganization of schooling must be undertaken. Schools must become nurturing and helpful instead of rule-bound warehouses of poorly motivated and rebellious students—who have come from damaged parents and sub-groups. It requires a whole different mentality with different goals. The attainment of personal power and wealth in itself must come to be seen as aberrant. Being considered an asset to the humanity of the society must take its place.

While the Trump phenomenon may be seen as obviously pathological, it also represents what happens when self-interest is allowed to run amok and eclipse all other values. In a large measure, narcissistic greed has been the driving force in too much of our development. Greed satisfies itself at the expense of everything else.   And it doesn't care.

Gopnik (2020) remarked:

> You know the rabbinical interpretation of why the Israelites had to wander in the desert for forty years?   It's because the older generation, born in slavery, had to [have time to] die off (p. 20).

It was thought the old people, stuck in their experience, would not be able to adjust to the context that was coming. Only young, more adaptable, people would be capable.

With the coronavirus and the disastrous American response to it, the system of narcissistic self-focus has finally been unmasked. It is time to begin to work toward a new kind of society. It must start with each one of us in terms of the issues we realize, how we assign our values, and how we treat each other.

REFERENCES

Coates, T-N. Between the World and Me. Spiegel and Grau, 2015.

Forsyth, D.R. The Psychology of Groups. https://nobaproject.com/modules/the-psychology-of-groups

Gabbard, G. O., Psychodynamic Psychiatry in Clinical Practice. AMA Press, 2014.

Gopnik, A. The Empty Couch. New Yorker, 06-01-2020.

Klein, E. America at the Breaking Point: The social upheaval of the 1960s meets the political polarization and institutional dysfunction of the present. Vox, 06-01-2020.

Lakoff, G. The Political Mind: A Cognitive Scientist's Guide to Your Brain and its Politics. Penguin, 2009.

Lakoff, G. Moral Politics: How Liberals and Conservatives Think. Third Edition. Chicago, 2016

Martin, G., and Pear, J. Behavior Modification. Tenth Edition. Pearson, 2014.

Menon, R. How the Pandemic Hit America. Salon, 07-18-2020.

Myers, A., and Hansen, C. H. Experimental Psychology. Seventh Edition. Cengage Learning, 2011

Rimm, D. C., and Masters, J.C. Behavior Therapy: Techniques and Empirical Findings. Academic Press, 1974.

Reviere, E. P. The Linked Self in Psychoanalysis: The Pioneering Work of Enrique Pichon Reviere, Eds.: Losso, R., De Setton, L. S., and Scharff, D. E. Routledge, 2017.

Rogers, C. The Carl Rogers Reader. Mariner, 1989.

Terry, W. S. Learning and Memory: Basic Principles, Processes, and Procedures. Fifth Edition. Routledge, 2017.

RACISM

On May 25, 2020, in Minneapolis, Minnesota, police officer Derek Chauvin, a White man, arrested George Floyd, a Black man, for attempting to pass a counterfeit $20.00 bill. During the arrest, Officer Chauvin placed his knee on the neck of Mr. Floyd who said, "I can't breathe." Officer Chauvin ignored this and kept his knee in place for over eight minutes during which time Mr. Floyd died. Three other officers assisted in the arrest, and none of them moved to help Mr. Floyd despite pleas from bystanders.

The reaction was swift and massive.

Major protests occurred in all major American cities and continued for weeks. The police had finally killed one Black man too many. The battle lines were clear to everyone in a stark light. America had a devastating race problem.

Awareness of a race problem was not new. From the beginning, America has battled and exploited people of color. The treatment of Native Americans is a blot worthy of immense shame. The treatment of Asian Americans during the Second World War is appalling. Hispanic people have been treated as enemies along the U.S. southern border.

But easily the darkest chapter in American history is the issue of slavery and how the after-effects of that period have been managed.

In 1860 Virginia adopted a slave code (see Lepore, 2020) which said in part:

> if any negroe or other slave shall absent himself from his masters service and lye hid and lurking in obscure places, committing injuries to the inhabitants, and shall resist any person or persons that shalby any lawful authority be employed to apprehend and take the said negroe, that then in case of such resistance, it shalbe lawful for such person or persons to kill the said negroe or slave soe lying out and resisting.

This perceived need to police the lives of Black people continued to be a focus ever since.

> Police patrolled Black neighborhoods and arrested Black people disproportionately; prosecutors indicted Black people disproportionately; juries found Black people guilty disproportionately; judges gave Black people disproportionately long sentences; and, then, after all this, social scientists, observing the number of Black people in jail, decided that, as a matter of biology, Black people were disproportionately inclined to criminality (Ibid).

In 1967 the Kerner Commission was appointed by President Johnson to research and analyze what had caused over 150 race riots in America. The Commission famously pointed out the United States was "moving toward two societies, one Black, one White—separate and unequal (Landrieu, 2020)." This report argued that racism had become institutionalized and had become a force for inequality.

This report was largely shelved, however, and no significant action was taken. Perhaps it was feared how this would be received by the White middle class. Countless other reports though the nation's history have met a similar fate. The problem has been pointed out over and over, but significant action has not been taken.

The result is, as the Kerner Commission suggested, an unequal society in which White people enjoy the fruits of America, and Black people get the crumbs—if that. Writers such as Baldwin (1974), Coates (2015), Morrison (2020), and Davis (1990, 2012) have argued that such a system negatively affects *both* White and Black people. The reason this is so is that both are *categories* and therefore *constructions*. This being the case, neither are allowed to simply be *persons*.

Further by participating blindly in the constructed system we have, both White and Black people contribute to it. Only the Black people, however, have been rebelling and demonstrating against this system. White people are just becoming aware of the magnitude of the problem. What is apparent is that the gap between White America and Black America is huge.

Structures in the American society that have kept the two groups apart include: the housing system, the criminal-justice system, the financial system, the education system, the health care system, and the political system. Racism is woven into the American society at its core.

In a wide sampling of research from several disciplines, Roberts and Rizzo (2020) suggested seven factors that contribute to American Racism: Organizing people into distinct groups by essentialist and normative reasoning. Factions that trigger in-group loyalty and inter-group competition and threat. Segregation. Racial hierarchy. Power and legislation bias. Media bias. Passivism which allows racism to "fester and persist."

Sharkey, Taylor, and Serkez (2020) pointed out that the unequal treatment of White and Black people is often the "result of policy choices." Effective effort has not been put into improving struggling neighborhoods beset by joblessness, poverty, environmental hazards, disease, drug abuse, and violence where many Black people live. Instead, White people have tended to segregate themselves in areas apart from such neighborhoods where schools are well-resourced, investment is made in public services, health care is readily available, and crime tends to be low.

The result of this is that the nation's most pressing social challenges are located in Black neighborhoods. Investing in bringing these neighborhoods into equal standing with White neighborhoods will require immense changes to the system. It has been estimated, for example, that during the coronavirus pandemic, less than half of Black adults have been able to keep their jobs. Black unemployment rates have routinely been almost ten percentage points higher than rates for Whites.

The number of White people with a bachelor's degree is two to three times higher than the number for Black people in many areas. The income disparity follows in course.

There are strong obstacles in the path for Black people to succeed and establish themselves. Race-restrictive housing policies have prevented home sales to minorities, banks have discriminated against people of color who have attempted to borrow money to by homes, and highways and public housing developments have been used to "solidify the boundaries of segregation (Ibid)."

Persistent racial gaps in home ownership are directly related to gaps in income. In many urban areas the gap between White homeownership and Black homeownership is over twenty percent and can be as high as fifty percent. This disparity is echoed in incarceration rates where rates for males who grew up in majority-Black neighborhoods is ten times higher than that among males who grew up in White-majority neighborhoods. Life expectancy can show a ten-year discrepancy. Data on the coronavirus pandemic showed higher rates of infection in people of color than among Whites. The availability of quality health-care, often dependent on income levels, is more difficult to find in minority areas.

When people in sub-standard areas rebel or riot over how they are treated, we call the police (our police), and we shoot them.

Clearly changes can be made to lessen the stratification of our society. Many of these changes include the establishment of policy that creates more inclusive communities.

Following the death of George Floyd, the American media focused increased attention on the fact people of color are so "disproportionately poor (Solomon, 2020)." It is clear that for each person killed by police, countless more are dying because of lack of employment, access to health care, and adequate social services. Economic oppression is obvious. Governments constantly plead lack of funds and an inability to offer any but token assistance.

Solomon (Ibid) claimed:

> But from city halls and state legislatures to corridors of power in Washington, the priorities that hold sway are largely imposed by leverage from big corporations and the wealthy who want their financial interests protected.

This amounts to a profit-driven war. In the past year, the city of Detroit spent $294 million dollars on the police and $9 million on health care (Ibid). At the same time there has been an enormous effort to separate racial justice from economic justice. According to the Brookings Institution (Ibid) "the net worth of a typical White family is nearly 10 times greater than that of a Black family." Much of this difference may be traced to wide differences in opportunity.

Solomon (Ibid) said:

> In effect, corporate capitalism has proven itself to be capable of methodical sadism in the pursuit of maximizing profits.

If this is the case, improvement in the lives of people of color involves a new approach to managing money in our society. Throughout our history White people have given themselves an advantage and have neglected, or actively worked against, Black people. This is the structure we have. It will persist until something is done to change it.

What will this entail?

Obviously White people will need to share their bounty. Such a thing begins in the mind. People who have succeeded in this system have used all their resources to help themselves get ahead and survive. These resources include both those that are innate as well as those that are situational (i.e., privilege). It is an uneven playing field.

In effect, this is a program of self-focus. I am using my resources for myself. What if it were expected I use a portion of my resources for others? What would that look like?

It would require a system that focused on the collective as well as the individual. The political system would have to be focused on lifting all boats instead of defeating the opposition. In effect, the opposition would be eliminated by not making such a distinction. Serious energy would have to be focused on less affluent areas and the availability of services in such areas.

In short, the culture would have to largely overcome its narcissism and greed. It would even help if the problem were widely acknowledged. "We are a culture of narcissism and greed!" It is all about me; screw everybody else! There is no need to worry about other people. I only care about myself.

It is hard to see how such a culture can think of itself as great. It is actually pathological.

Since our culture is so heavily invested in power and money, it is these areas that will be the most resistant to change. This will become the locus of the culture war, not race. Complete change is not necessary. Profit for myself might morph to profit for myself plus help for others.

The element of empathy, which involves feeling-with another instead of feeling-for another (Mitleid), is routinely severely damaged or missing outright in narcissistic personalities. This is a defining element. Narcissistic persons show little or no remorse for the effects of their actions on other people. They only care about themselves.

It is this personality disorder the American system has enabled in its political and corporate structures. The accumulation of wealth and power is regarded as proof of superiority. But, clearly, this is not the case. It is the absence of empathy that is the psychological problem. Without empathy wealth and power become destructive.

In an address to behavioral scientists, Martin Luther King, Jr. (1968) said:

Thus, it may well be that our world is in dire need of a new organization, The International Association for the Advancement of Creative Maladjustment. Men and women should be as maladjusted as the prophet Amos, who in the midst of the injustices of his day, could cry out in words that echo across the centuries, 'Let justice roll down like waters and righteousness like a mighty stream'; or as maladjusted as Abraham Lincoln, who in the midst of his vacillations finally came to see that this nation could not survive half slave and half free; or as maladjusted as Thomas Jefferson, who in the midst of an age amazingly adjusted to slavery, could scratch across the pages of history, words lifted to cosmic proportions, 'We hold these truths to be self-evident, that all men are created equal. That they are endowed by their creator with certain inalienable rights. And that among these are life, liberty, and the pursuit of happiness.' And through such creative maladjustment, we may be able to emerge from the bleak and desolate midnight of man's inhumanity to man, into the bright and glittering daybreak of freedom and justice.

Narcissistic structure begins in the experiences of childhood (Kohut, 1984). There is an absence of empathy in the childhood home. The child does not feel heard or genuinely considered. He or she does not feel parents are concerned about his or her feelings. The child is essentially living in a person-less world, in the sense that interpersonal resonance is missing—or is dangerous. Caring about oneself alone is what is on display. No one cares about anybody else.

This pattern of interacting is present in the very air of the family home in much the same way one's native language is present. It is the way people do things—the way things are done. It is learned naturally. Learning something else in such an environment would be odd. Besides, it is all the child knows. Other childhood experiences are for other children.

Further, it is likely this pattern is also noticed outside the home. At school. In church. In retail shops and on sidewalks and highways. Everyone is out for him or herself. The child, naturally, wants to matter in this system. The way you do that, the child is told, is to get the best grades, do the best at hop-scotch or baseball, achieve, achieve, achieve—don't worry about the others. Be the best at whatever you do. This is the purpose of life.

It is a bit like learning the irregular German verbs.

Further, *our* people are on this side of town. *Those* people are on the other. Our people attend this church. Those people attend another. Our family has dinner with management people. Those people dine with workers, &c.

Such stratified inequality creates rage. It is hard to be left out of the best group. Everyone knows you are inferior. Soon, degrees of acceptability develop. "Well, I am more acceptable than you are." Every little bit helps in an exclusionary system.

Poor White people who lack significant education have been able to point to their relative standing vis a vis Black people. When conditions begin to improve for Black people, this group of White people are threatened. Thinking themselves to be the "true" Americans (narcissism), they seek to keep colored people "in their place."

Poor White people have not, as a rule, had even moderately easy lives. This is true even without the negative light in which they are seen in our culture. Largely ostracized into their own groups and areas, they are left to their own devices. This is a self-repeating pattern that continually renews itself.

When the admired levels of society carry such weight, the border around them tends to be vigorously patrolled. Too many people in any given level lessens its value. Stratification is required.

None of this is necessarily set in stone. Narcissistic people can be helped to improve in many cases. There is no reason a narcissistic culture cannot be helped as well. The first step is typically for a person (or a culture) to realize there is a problem and seek help. In a psychotherapeutic context, the issue can be understood, and steps can be taken to work it through. But the first step is seeking treatment.

In psychological terms, the American culture needs help. The recent riots over the death of a Black man are a symptom of the disease. The disease is narcissism and non-empathic self-focus.

In Utah emphasis is placed on having the "right" values. These are the values of the LDS church. Adhering to these values is considered good. Not adhering to them is considered bad. The game is simple: we are good; you are bad. This game is played in school, in the workplace, and in the local media. LDS people don't, as a rule, think of their behavior as creating a problem. They are only trying to do as they should. Rejecting others is only reasonable. They don't share our values. Besides, we have the political power, and we can conduct affairs as we wish.

The God that is projected is a strict-father God. Obedience is highly valued. Individual creativity, not so much. Here, it is not individual people who are the problem as much as the structure of the organization. By dividing people into us and them, the system maintains prejudice. By granting favors to us and not to them, the system splits the culture in two. In this system, we will prevail, and you will be cast out.

No one says, "My own activity is negatively impacting an entire group of people." But it does. Membership in such an organization places one alongside those who maintain the social split.

In much the same way, many White Americans have not deliberately set out to harm another group of people. But their membership in a system that does just that is a problem. It is important for White Americans to realize their culpability—through little thought of their own—in making life so miserable for so many. No one is innocent. It is time for the therapist.

REFERENCES

Coates, T-N, Between the World and Me. Spiegel and Grau, 2015.

Davis, A. Women, Culture, and Politics. Vintage, 1990.

Davis, A. The Meaning of Freedom: And Other Difficult Dialogues. City Lights Open Media, 2012.

Hill, E., Tiefenthaler, A. Triebert, C., Jones, D., Willis, H., and Stein, R. 8 Minutes and 46 Seconds: How George Floyd was Killed in Police Custody. New York Times, 05-31-2020.

King, M. L. Jr. The Role of the Behavioral Scientist in the Civil Rights Movement. Journal of Social Issues, Vol. 24, No. 1, 1968.

Kohut, H. How does Analysis Cure? Chicago, 1984.

Landrieu M. The Price We Have Paid for Not Confronting Racism. New York Times, 06-03-2020.

Lepore, J. The Long Blue Line: Inventing the Police. New Yorker, 20-07-2020.

Morrison, T. The Source of Self-Regard: Selected Essays, Speeches, and Meditations. Vintage International, 2020.

Roberts, S.O., and Rizzo, M.T. The Psychology of Ame ican Racism. American Psychologist, June, 2020.

Sharkey, P., Taylor, K-Y, and Serkez, Y. The Gaps Between White and Black America, in Charts. New York Times, 06-19-2020.

Solomon, N. Corporate Media is Focusing on Racism at Last—but Ducking Economic Injustice. Salon, 06-13-2020.

GREED

America has long been a capitalistic society. Manufac-
turers make things, and we buy them. There is always a
demand for the supply. Optimally this pattern rests on an
assumption that a portion of profits will be re-invested
into operations to benefit the public by creating jobs, services, and income.

The United States was a beacon of the world following
the second world war. It stood for democracy, freedom,
and the rule of law. Though never perfect—it had a brutal and dehumanizing racism problem—it at least spoke
for fairness. Parents told their (White) children the ge-
nius of America was that anyone could work his or her

way up in the system. Though the playing field was never entirely equal, the opportunity of the American Dream was always assumed to be in place.

This assumption of the American Dream is false. Increasingly social mobility as well as median wages have declined. Recent children expect to make less than their parents. The resulting gap between the rich and the poor and the old and the young has been largely ignored by policymakers and investors.

In today's world, the postal code where you were born can account for up to two thirds of the wealth you may earn (Leonhardt, 2020). Growing disparity is due to a span of policy negligence where credit and monetary stimulus shortcuts have been enacted instead of fundamental reform. The result of this is that capitalism has been extremely successful in generating wealth but poor at its distribution.

The present, largely Republican, government is hostile to the core American values of democracy, freedom, and the rule of law. The distribution of income is exceptionally unequal.

For a period following the second world war American society operated in terms of a relative balance between labor and management. Unions were strong and workers' issues were represented in corporate hallways. Lind (2020) argued that this stability began to erode in the nineteen seventies when a managerial elite began to make decisions on its own. Technical issues, profit potential, global trade agreements, and a focus on efficiency increasingly drove decisions instead of what was good for workers.

Further, a new ethic took place in which trade unions, individual legislatures, as well as grass-roots religious and civic institutions were weakened or bypassed. Those hardest hit by these developments were workers without college degrees.

According to Leonhardt (Ibid.) the economists Case and Deaton (see 2020) chronicled deaths of despair that dramatically increased not only among White working-class Americans but extended to those without a four-year college degree:

> In the early 1990s, the number of white adults without a college education who died from drug overdoses, alcoholism or suicide was fairly low—and the death rates for younger adults were lower than for older adults.
>
> But over the past three decades, deaths of despair among whites without a college degree—especially those under age 50— have soared (Leonhardt, Ibid).

Death rates for White people with a college degree during the same period have risen only a little and are lower for young people than for the old.

This is a trend that is not seen in Europe during the same period.

> European countries have faced the same kind of technological change we have, and they're not seeing their people killing themselves with guns or drugs or alcohol…there is something unique about the way the U.S. is handling this (Ibid).

These authors point out inequality has risen more in the U.S, and middle-class incomes have decreased farther, than in France, Germany or Japan.

Also during this period large corporations have increased their market share and outsourcing has become a norm. These developments encourage executives to view low-wage workers as an expense. Added to this is the fact the American health care system is the world's most expensive, though it has not been able to keep many people healthy. Non-college Whites are also less likely to remain married or to attend church.

Meanwhile the richest ten percent of Americans take home forty eight percent of domestic income (Kahloon, 2020). Also Piketty (2014) drew attention to problems in this approach by comparing the economic share of the top one percent of people with that of everyone else. Piketty found that over the past century the rate of return on capital owned by the rich had exceeded the growth rate of the economy (r>g). That is, wealth is largely flowing to the rich.

In a new book Piketty (2020) argues that the levels of inequality we get are those of which we approve.

Said Kahloon (2020):

> [Piketty] argues that the 'Brahmin left'—the most educated citizens and the greatest beneficiaries of the knowledge economy and the supposed meritocracy—has captured the left-wing parties in Western democracies, distracting those parties from their mission of improving the lives of working people. Conservative parties, meanwhile, are under the sway of the "merchant right." Such polarization makes debate over redistribution impossible, and so the lower classes debate [issues like] immigration and borders instead (p. 77).

Clearly the amassing of increased wealth has become a runaway obsession in its own right.

It is impossible not to notice the familiar scent of greed in all of this. It is as if there is no end to our hunger for more and more, as if we are somehow caught in a giant whirlwind that has us spinning so fast we no longer know what we are doing.

There is something exciting in excess. We are surrounded by wealth and opportunity, open sex and intoxication, violence, and religious belief. Our capitalist culture needs us to want the products it produces, and we are beset by a steady drumbeat of advertising, trade shows, window displays, and print circulars. The only place in some towns where people may gather is the local shopping center where consumption, even blind consumption, is encouraged.

In such a climate the excesses of other people are disturbing to us as they threaten to awaken a realization that we too have become creatures of excess. The ordinary is no longer good enough. Yet our reactions to the excesses of other people reveal to us what our conflicts are.

It is in our fantasies where we are most excessive. We dream in grand and unlimited terms. It is not in reality where we wish to eat everything—eating too much in reality is painful. Non-stop excitement or violence becomes destructive.

Psychoanalytic theories have considered the origins of greed. Hobbesian in his thinking, Freud felt we were naturally a swirling mass of sex and aggression that had to be civilized in order to survive (see Jones, 1961). He also held that money was primitively related to filth, and that its value had been transformed by reaction formation. Klein (1932) held that greed was a part of human nature that was unavoidably self-destructive. Klein thought we project this destructiveness onto the outside world in the form of acquisitiveness, envy, and hate. Kohut (1984) felt that greed comes from not getting enough love or affirmation in one's childhood. When children don't get enough affection and empathy, they develop a life-long emptiness which they constantly attempt to fill.

Winnicott (1958) held that greed is a primitive love impulse. It is greed, experienced as unrefined passion and desire, that allows the child to differentiate between love and hate. Winnicott (Ibid), however, made a distinction between greed and greediness. Greed is a primitive impulse for love, whereas greediness is ruthless and potentially antisocial. A child who experiences emotional deprivation resorts to a desperate attempt to get rid of the anxiety resulting from this. In this way greed is life-affirming, whereas greediness is destructive.

It is hard not to think there is some significant hunger behind greediness and rampant acquisitiveness. Our fantasies tell us we would be happy with a new car, a new dress, a higher salary, but we are oddly surprised when such things don't yield the happiness we imagined.

Wachtel (2003) wrote:

> At some level, I think, most Americans are aware that something is awry in the kind of consumerism that our society spawns...[This includes] the potentially irreversible damage we are doing to the environment in our relentless pursuit of what we think is the good life; the vast inequalities we are generating; the way we are increasingly rationing health care, sup-

posedly because we 'can't afford' more extensive coverage, even while our roads are increasingly crammed with huge and expensive SUVs. Our homes—and *second* homes—are 50% larger than the homes people lived in in the affluent 1950s and 1960s. In this context, I would like to invite reflection on…well conducted studies [that indicate] economic success plays a strikingly small role in people's sense of happiness or well-being…

A prime image of this unrestrained acquisitiveness is seen in the 1987 film *Wall Street*. Here Gordon Gekko argues:

> The point is, ladies and gentlemen, greed is good. Greed works, greed is right, greed clarifies, cuts through, and captures the essence of the evolutionary spirit. Greed in all its forms, greed for life, money, love, knowledge has marked the upward curve of mankind.

Greed, of course, is scarcely a new phenomenon. The age of the robber barons at the end of the nineteenth century produced vast wealth. But at that time only the wealthy could be greedy. Increasingly in modern America, greed has become the province of the entire society. Large portions of the society have come to believe every problem can be solved by the markets. Liberal education has become almost quaint and outdated. MBA programs, meanwhile, grow in scope. Focus on materialism becomes central (see Coutu, 2003).

Yet, American society has not only become greedy in materialism alone. We have become focused on ourselves to the exclusion of other countries. We want only the best schools for our children. We want our religious beliefs to exclude all other beliefs. We want to be the best. On top. We want it all for ourselves.

Somehow in all this passion we forgot a bit who we are. We began pulling alone, against even those we knew. Our sense of community wobbled and leaned over. It is everyone for him or herself on our freeways, in our shopping centers, on busy sidewalks.

No one could miss the terrible hunger lurking behind all this struggle. No one could ignore the sense of emptiness. Perhaps we are a country that has focused too little on taking care of what is precious and human. Psychology tells us it began at home in our childhoods.

Empathic resonance has been less valued than achievement. Feelings have been less valued than behavior. If this were not the case, we would be emotional empathizers instead of behaving accumulators. We would have small moments for each other. We would have the ego strength *not* to consume—as we would not need possessions to signify our worth. Having known loving empathy, we would already be of worth.

Instead we have been left only able to compete and struggle against each other. Our lives have become difficult. Our children enter a culture that is foreboding and threatening. Class and educational lines are increasingly pre-set. Wealth is increasingly pre-arranged. We are increasingly separated in groups that do not interact with other groups—or we even despise them.

This is not the direction of greatness.

It has long been known that the attempt to make up for an inner emptiness is often managed through external acquisition. If one is bored, the solution is to buy something. If one is sad, the solution is the same. Whatever the inner issue might be, acquiring some external thing will make it better. It is a clever trick—but it doesn't work. I will still be the same unhappy person I am in a new car as I was in the old one. I may have a fabulous wardrobe, but be miserable. But look at all those happy people in the advertisements! I want to be happy like them. On their boat. At their party. I want people to know I am somebody important.

Soon I have amassed a collection of fine things but have no one with whom to share them. No one is interested in fawning over my great stuff. It seems all I have is stuff. Without it, I am a rather plain person.

The healthy way to correct for inner emptiness, or an inner sense of inadequacy, is to work through the origins of such feelings. It is likely I have been deprived of something in my life, and it is this deprivation that needs to be understood so that the wound it created may be healed. Refusing to heal the inner problem and trying to cover it up with external compensation won't work. I will end up with stuff plus an inner wound—scarcely the outcome I wished.

When a handful of people own as much wealth as the entire rest of the society combined, it is clear something has gone significantly wrong. That I am able to sleep in my silk sheets while large numbers of people don't have enough to eat, suggests a catastrophic failure of empathy. But this is not the only problem. I am dedicated to the task of doubling my holdings. I want more.

It is only when I am dissevered from meaningful connection with other people that I can ignore them and give my full concentration to myself. Yet in this society such behavior is in accord with the cultural ethos. We want money. Money buys everything. I would rather be rich and depressed than poor and depressed. I want to be admired.

Humanity itself is absent in such reasoning. Humanity is also absent in a culture built on such reasoning. Humanity-schumanity. I want a full wardrobe, an imported sports car, and a world cruise. That would be the good life.

Krugman (2020) wrote of the American right wing:

> You see, the modern U.S. right is committed to the proposition that greed is good, that we're all better off when indi-

viduals engage in the untrammeled pursuit of self-interest. In their vision, unrestricted profit maximization by businesses and un-regulated consumer choice is the recipe for a good society…Many on the right are en-raged at any suggestion that their actions should take other people's welfare into account.

A culture that supports such desires and does not notice or care about the suffering of persons left without is a wounded culture. It is a culture in which human consid-eration and tenderness is sorely lacking. The presence of one empathic person improves an entire block. Greed de-bases it.

Economic growth created from greed ben-efits the prospering few and does not trickle into the pockets of the poor.... These condi-tions create a greed driven culture, infec-tious like a virus, causing markets to spiral out of control. The lure to greed also en-dangers the mental health of the poor who experience needless suffering and neglect from being deprived of their needs (Nikelly, 2006, p. 67).

Also:

It seems that greed is everywhere, not that it always hasn't been everywhere, but now it has taken on new dimensions, risen to new heights.... The consequence of this has been a far reaching economic, and social calamity that touches us all. The damage to the individual and society, however, goes beyond the actual financial losses, which have been substantial, to the often devastating subjective meanings of the losses for the individual, and the destructive influence of the highly visible financially successful but morally corrosive sub-cultures that stimulate greed and envy (Winarick, , pp. 317-318).

Popular media glamorizes the lives of the rich and famous. We are dazzled by images of their homes, their cars, their possessions as indicators of the good life. It is significant we do not see accounts of the broken and distorted lives such people often lead behind such images, the heartache and misery that is suffered in such splendid surroundings.

Meanwhile the situation for low income workers is dire. These people are routinely overlooked as a group in need though they are the people who are performing the tasks that keep society going. This has especially been true during the coronavirus pandemic.

Stansbury and Summers (2020) remarked:

The American economy has become more ruthless, as declining unionization, increasingly demanding and empowered shareholders, decreasing real minimum wages, reduced worker protections, and the increases in outsourcing domestically and abroad have disempowered workers—with profound consequences for the labor market and the broader economy.

These low earning workers have been called "essential employees." They include: hospital orderlies, trash collectors, grocery workers, as well as food delivery drivers, paramedics, mortuary technicians, and postal, shipping, maintenance, wastewater treatment, truck-stop and mass-transit employees. Forty-four percent of workers aged eighteen to sixty-four are low wage workers. These people are disproportionately people of color (Edsall, 2020).

One of the issues complicating attempts to increase minimum wages for these groups is the appeal of replacing (increasingly) expensive workers with automation including artificial intelligence.

On the other hand, progress is possible in terms of making it easier for private-sector workers to unionize, strengthening the educational system, including technical training, lowering incarceration rates, and adjustments to the minimum wage.

A significant improvement could be made if management were to concern itself with the well-being of its workers in addition to profit. It is this stripping away of human concern in favor of maximizing profit that has crippled the capitalist system and created runaway income disparity.

Even more important is the fact we now live in a society that ignores the well-being of almost half its population to the benefit of the very top.

In psychological terms this is a sick system. It creates conflict and anguish by its very nature. The system needs intervention at its core. When human well-being is considered in addition to wealth and power, priorities shift. This, in turn, requires shareholders—you and I—to allow management to include human concerns. When we try to maximize our own return, we thereby make life more difficult for a huge class of people.

We, ourselves, are the people who want more and more and more. Ours is a system that is coming apart. A commitment to human decency must be made.

REFERENCES

Case, A. and Deaton, A. Deaths of Despair and the Future of Capitalism. Princeton, 2020.

Coates, T-N, Between the World and Me. Spiegel and Grau, 2015.

Edsall, T.B., Why Do We Pay So Many People So Little Money? New York Times, 06-24-2020.

Kahloon, I. The Leveler: Thomas Piketty goes global in "Capital and Ideology." New Yorker, 03-09-2020.

Klein, M. The Psychoanalysis of Children. Hogarth, 1932.

Krugman, P. The Cult of Selfishness is Killing America. New York Times, 07-27-2020.

Leonhardt, D. Commentary: Working-class life is killing Americans. The Telegraph, 03-17-2020.

Lind, M. The New Class War: Saving Democracy from the Managerial Elite. Portfolio, 2020.

Nikelly, A. The Pathogenesis of Greed: Causes and Consequences. International Journal of Applied Psychoanalytic Studies, 2006.

Stansbury, A., and Summers, L.H. The Declining Worker Power Hypothesis. See Edsall, T.B. Why Do We Pay Po Many People So Little Money? New York Times, 06-24-2020.

Wachtel, P.L. Full Pockets, Empty Lives: A Psychoanalytic Exploration of the Culture of Greed. American Journal of Psychoanalysis, 2003.

Winarick, K. Thoughts on Greed and Envy. American Journal of Psychoanalysis, 2010.

Winnicott, D. W. Collected Papers: Through Pediatrics to Psychoanalysis. Basic. 1958.

CONSTRUCTIONS

> Late yestre'en I saw the new moon
> With the old moon in her arms,
> And I fear, I fear, my dear master,
> That we will come to harm
>
> Ballad of Sir Patrick Spence
> 13th Century

The comedian Jerry Seinfeld imagined a town that had a hero who played for the home team, wearing the home team jersey. Townspeople cheered and rooted for him. He then got a lucrative offer and moved to the team of a rival. After this, he returned to the original town for a game wearing the jersey of its rival, and the townspeople booed him. Seinfeld quipped "they were rooting for laundry."

What is ours is ours. What is not is not. It is how we know who we are and how we define ourselves. Jerseys matter. Icons signal our position, place, and persuasion. Labels are so important, they mean more than what they label.

It is no laughing matter. If you don't belong, it is hard to survive. When your own group does not accept you as one of them, you are seen as other—one of *those*—out there. We have been raised this way since elementary school. Those who don't fit are tormented and given no harbor. It is, of course, possible to thrive as an outlier, but you have to have some quality that allows such a position to work. Without such a quality, there is no hope for you here.

This is the tyranny of the group. Within groups there routinely becomes a struggle for rank or position. Some people rise in the group's esteem while some fall. This is important, because those who rise can attract followers who also want to be seen as associated with those who rise instead of the fallen. This leads to power.

Like a tug-of-war, beta baboons challenge alpha baboons for dominion. Sometimes they win, and the power shifts. The struggle may become all consuming.

Just as families and social structures can be modeled either on a strict father pattern or a nurturing parent pattern, so groups may be seen this way. In some groups the leader gives the rules, and the others follow. The focus is on obedience. In other groups input and suggestions are solicited from all members. The focus is on inclusion.

Human history is filled with accounts of tyrants and abuses of power. In fact, it is difficult to keep systems from moving in this direction. Yet history is also filled with accounts of the fall of tyrants and systems of power. In evolutionary terms, the most adaptive individuals are those most flexible.

Once power is established it must be defended. When the city-state was developed in ancient societies, armies were required to keep other city-states from plundering one's own.

Yet what would happen if we were to shift sides—if only as an exercise? What would we be able to see that we couldn't see before? Would we see the other side is as limited as we are?

We may learn the task of getting all the way free of some pervasive influence is difficult. Some little piece always remains to trip us up. This is a special struggle for those raised in privilege. Is awareness of the privilege enough? Is renouncing the privilege enough?

The problem occurs, because the context always tells us a lie. It tells us it contains all that needs to be known. It fills up all the life we are able to see. This lie will hold until we are able to leave the context. Of course there are contexts we can leave as well as contexts we cannot leave.

Still, leaving comes with a cost. In Giovanni's Room, Baldwin (2013) said: "You don't have a home until you leave it, and then, when you have left it, you never can go back." You don't have a home, because you can now see where that home is situated in the larger reality. You can't go back, because the world is wider now. Home can never be enough, and this will gnaw at you, because you realize no place is enough, and no place can be a home the way you once conceived of home.

Soon life sums to zero. How terribly difficult it is to find one's own history small. The past seems like a great collusion of people whose mission it was to lead one astray with solemn seriousness. And then, when one had long moved beyond them, how limited and small they seemed, how limited to the context one has now moved beyond.

Then, for one, there can be no ending. The prices paid lead to a kind of isolation, because one cannot remain in any place. Nor is there an identity that can stick—except possibly: seeker.

What is the price of not belonging anywhere? Of always being considered wrong. How far can one reach with one's hours?

The occupation of seeking is always in danger of throwing too much away. Since the focus is always on the not-yet-discovered, the focus is not on the already-found. And some of the already-found is priceless and pure. I think all of a sudden of the San Frediano Basilica in Lucca, Italy. How powerfully it spoke to me. How elemental it was and serene. I still can only imagine it empty. The silence it speaks.

And it is that silence that speaks to me, has become a part of me. I don't know what to say to people. So I meet them at their level. I nod. I understand. But I am not there really. I am in Lucca at night when lights are on the frescoes above the door. The streets are empty and beautiful as they never are where I live. And whatever it is that is alive there, is welcoming. And only those left out on the streets late find it. Or does it find them?

Andre Gide wrote: It is better to be hated for what you are than to be loved for what you are not.

Think of God. The notion of God is a personification of love in the universe. God is the good parent. Children of abuse cannot find him. Religions that get hung up in rules instead of acceptance and tolerance cannot find him. The poor do it the best—and the artists. Artists spend their time doing what God does: creating. It is important to create. Even if no one likes what one creates. It is how to be closest to God.

Even the name God is objectionable. It is a name taken over by those who wish to be right instead of belonging with those who do not need to be right, those who are capable of sustained uncertainty. As Pascal noted: Uncertainty is the only evidence we have for growth.

There is something to be said for insecure attachment. Bowlby (1988) thought that the familiar is equated with safety. This is why change is so difficult: it moves outward, into the unsafe. So, what sort of damn fool would go out there, beyond safety and what is familiar? What kind of fool would *want* to go out there?

Change is the order of life. Nothing is static. Life itself is a continual unfolding, an opening to what lies beyond here. The pain of growth is movement. This requires a tolerable level of pain. Harlow's monkeys (1971) were overwhelmed by what was new. Fear is okay if it can somehow be struggled through.

As a stream of water finds its way in the dirt, so searching inches ahead. To find safety? No. To get used to inching ahead. Life on the outside. The grace of great things.

The work of Pichon Riviere (2017) focuses on the interpersonal connection between two individuals. Riviere called this the *link*. The link is formed in three dimensions: mind, body, and interaction. They exist in the intermediate area between inner and outer constructions and form a kind of shared, interpersonal, construction that modifies each member involved in the link.

Both external relations and mental representations are thus formed both by the individual unconscious as well as by external relations.

The problem is too many of us are stopped at the start. As we try to learn about and find a way in the world we have just discovered, we run into a door that has been slammed shut. If we are lucky enough to have caretakers who are genuinely able to find us—instead of only finding their image of us, or the us they need us to be for them—we have a chance to be seen and develop as real persons. If, however, we are not seen or our lives don't genuinely matter in their own right to our caregivers, we are forced to develop a buffer to such caregivers.

If I get the sense my parents don't really care about finding out who I am, they become unavailable to me as aids in my growth. Yet I need them. They heat the house and put food on the table. This puts me in an untenable situation. I cannot give voice to my anger and disappointment in them, because I need the attachment I have to them. It is at this point I must begin to tune out essential elements in reality. It is when I turn away.

Imagine a lantern. One side of the lantern is clear to allow light to emerge, and the other side is opaque preventing light from emerging. When the child is feeling good, alert, well fed, and accepted, he or she turns the clear side to reality, thus illuminating things in the world. When the child is frightened or overwhelmed, he or she turns the opaque side to reality, thus gating out input and illuminating the self. In such a fashion a child may learn to spend more time in reality or away from reality in the self.

If the caretakers are truly frightening or neglectful, the child must develop a system to *protect* him or her from others. A major problem with this is the child is too young to be faced with such an enormous project entirely on his or her own.   The self becomes a mask behind which the child seeks to control others in his or her life so as not to be hurt. That is, the child *pretends* to be present but is actually "safe" behind the mask-barrier. The child is never truly present.

The logic is simple: it is better to be away from a dangerous situation than to be in it. If, however, I can't truly escape the dangerous situation, it is better to be buffered from it.

There are several problems with this approach however—though it *does* enable me to "survive" the impossible situation. The biggest problem is it stunts my growth. I am no longer interacting with and growing in the world straightaway. It is my mask that is interacting with the world and then only in an attempt to minimize hurt. Another problem with this is I am never available for close interpersonal interactions. Only my mask does this.

This is an extreme case, but none of us had perfect parents, nor are any of us perfect parents. Our capacity to genuinely involve ourselves in the world and others is always a matter of degree. Furthermore, without this capacity to genuinely involve ourselves, part of our energy is always used in managing old hurts and dealing with incapable others—either in person or in our minds. If all I have known is hurt, disappointment, or neglect it will be hard for me to see others in other than hurtful, disappointing, or neglecting ways. It will even be my view of the world.

A self that is buffered against a world is importantly cut off from it. Furthermore, such a self cuts itself off when the world is seen as intolerably threatening. It is, in a sense, a self frozen in time. It is also a self that relates to its view of the world instead of relating to the world openly.

The result is a catastrophic lack of curiosity as well as a resistance to change. It is easier to protect a limited space that is unchanging than to grow and expand. Besides, growth and expansion creates anxiety as it moves one beyond what is familiar in the search for new horizons.

This is how the strict father is formed. Such a person sets up his domain (his fortress) and requires his family to live within its perimeter. What is beyond the perimeter is, by definition, rejected as threatening. An entire culture can be based on this logic and view itself as the only correct (true) culture.

With enough power such a culture can limit what it sees and is required to manage. That is, the focus narrows. Deviations from the culture's views are threatening and therefore not allowed and punished. The past is seen as a superior time partly because it is past—and therefore not alive and threatening as is the present.

The mental health of such a culture is severely compromised. If mental health involves being able to successfully deal with the world, the closed down culture is crippled, as it is only able to deal with a reduced scope of the world—and then only on the group's terms.

The authority of the strict father to establish the rules and police compliance to them is constantly under threat. This is why it is so rigidly defended. Without such authority the closed down group could not be held in place and would gradually adapt to an unfettered world. That is to say children raised in a closed down group find rules emphasized, whereas children in an open group learn how to stand on their own feet and cope with events as they come along. For this latter group there is no right way. There are ways of varying degrees of adequacy.

To maintain authority the strict father must have power. Those under him must be forced or intimidated. Deviants must be hurt.

The history of the human race is filled with power people who unleashed untold suffering in the service of maintaining their power. Wars have been fought to see who had the most power. Those doing the fighting were fodder. Those who lost power were subsumed.

Where there was no power in play, the world operated according to its natural rhythms. Seen in this light the history of power is the history of weakness and fear. Human history becomes a sad and bloody tale of the effects of human smallness, interspersed with attempts to discover and grow.

It continues today. As Freud (see Jones, 1961) realized the forces of growth and resistance struggle continually to prevail. Even concepts of God have gotten into the act. Some describe a strict father deity, whereas others describe a nurturing parent deity. Many have given up on concepts of deity as being encrusted by religions claiming authority and truth.

Clearly, in terms of healthy functioning, autocracy has run its course. This, however, is not yet realized in day to day culture and the workplace where hierarchies remain and flourish. Such hierarchies are rarely geared to maximize health and well-being. They are geared to profit and output.

It is for us, as individuals, to find our way in this terrain. It is for us to become agents of well-being instead of agents of resistance and fear. The world we have now has brought us crushing inequality, a damaged planet, and widespread human misery. This is scarcely a prescription for greatness.

The construct of power and wealth, of being better and triumphant has led us into darkness. A construct of welcome, help, and consideration struggles beside it. This is a concept of one in the middle of the other. The psychology is different as is the outcome. Dominance is traded for inclusion and welcome. Evolution itself favors flexibility over rigidity.

It is important to stop punishing children for being wrong. It is better to help students than to rank them. The scramble for top billing is too expensive. There is more capacity in the entire group of strivers than there is in the top dog.

II

The American culture that relegates non-White, straight males, such as Blacks, women, and LGBTQ+ people, among others, to secondary status is destructive to the society in general. To significantly impact millions of lives, because White males desire to feel superior is an arrogant failure of basic humanity. This is a culture that must be left behind.

The narcissistic symptoms of entitlement and self-focus betray a self that has been severely damaged. The lack of working empathy itself indicates significant interpersonal developmental trauma. That our culture is apparently unable to realize the extent to which such people are compromised is unsettling.

For a group to be seriously considered, enough people must deem that group worthy of significant importance to the collective whole for this to take place. This requires the group to attain enough of a voice to be heard by the larger collective. Countless groups struggle for this consideration at all times. The collective, however, is not a monolith. It has numerous factions and subsets that sometimes actively oppose each other. Thus some subsets may hear a group which raises its voice, and other subsets may ignore or rebel against it.

History books present different accounts in California than they do in Texas (Goldstein, 2020). The California texts emphasize equality and inclusion. The Texas texts elide these issues. Students in these states are presented with differing accounts of what is important to their country. Thus different voices are heard. Who decides?

Clearly such decisions emanate from the collective in each state. They are a manifestation of power in that other voices also strive for inclusion but are pushed aside. What, we may ask, are the motivations of groups who make the decisions? Do they wish all voices to be heard? Only some voices? Only the voice of their particular group?

Soon this battle between voices becomes a battle for the minds of people, for their concept of the world in which they live. And their neighbors will likely agree with their view, having been similarly taught. Wherever they go in their daily lives, the same tune may be on the jukebox. It is "how things are." But it isn't. Three states away, the voices are different, and people are taught a different concept.

In addition to *what* views one is taught, one is also taught, or it is suggested, what the ontological status of the view is. That is, is it one view among many? Or is it the only correct (true) view? Do other views deserve to be heard? Or is this the only view allowed?

Much of this debate is informed by childrearing practices described above. Is one taught to be open to new information or closed to it? Does the parent (the authority) decide the right answer or is the child rewarded for seeking after it?

The interesting factor in this difference involves the presence or absence of threat. It may be said natural curiosity goes where it can go without penalty. Since childhood, natural curiosity has been encouraged or discouraged. It has also been modeled or not, valued or not. The desire to know and experience pushes outward, or it is stifled.

Seen in this light openness and curiosity become mental health issues. It is a matter of according others genuine consideration versus according consideration only to a select few. In a way it is a matter of being a citizen of the world or a citizen of a neighborhood. And since childrearing is largely a function of parenting, one's parents have a significant hand in shaping the kind of child one will be.

Helping a child to be as mentally and emotionally capable as he or she can be is as important as helping a child to be physically healthy. Children who are open to the world have a leg up on children who are closed—if for no other reason than they are adaptable to more contexts and therefore have more options. Children who have primarily had but one, or few, experience(s) are far less equipped for the world we have, as the world is constantly changing and rearranging itself.

It may be argued there a millions of jobs that require obedience. Are there?

Certainly there are millions of jobs that are routine, repetitive, and boring. Do these jobs require obedience, or do they require an ability to perform in a routine way?

Are managers of workers required to be autocratic, or can they be helpful and encouraging? Is punishment the only tool for eliciting appropriate behavior?

Obviously not. Obedience may be achieved by punishment and threat, or it may be achieved by helpfulness and incentive. This latter option may require a bit more effort on the part of managers, but the rewards it brings are significant.

III

The American culture is currently struggling to grow up and take its place in a more mature world. The Trump era was a time of vigorous efforts made against notions of democracy, even in some cases embracing fascism. Some of the responsibility for these efforts can be laid at the feet of elites who ignored, manipulated, and denigrated the poor, the working class, the rural, and lesser educated people. As a result, these people got mad.

They should have. Exclusion is the opposite of a welcoming society, and denying people a voice is contrary to the essence of democracy. Still, this is not the whole picture. The slow progress civilization has made in the world has been progress in the face of tyranny, exploitation, and repression. All of this has been managed in the name of power.

This is not to say virtue is to be found in office buildings or professional societies. It is not. People, however, become angry when they are abused or hurt. They despair when there is no hope. Conversely, people improve when they are helped, unless they have been too broken.

The attempt by those with White male racial politics to hang on to a world that has disappeared—even to the extent of destroying democracy—indicates a form of selfish self-focus that equals the selfish self-focus on the part of elites that angered them in the first place. It is incumbent on us to do better than this.

What is becoming obsolete in the world is the urge to dominate by power. Typically described as a masculine impulse, the struggle for power has been responsible for great human suffering and destruction. It is simply not worth it. Finding a way to get along with each other and help each other flourish is a worthy goal.

The logic here is that, while it may be impossible to change the character of the world, one can change oneself.

REFERENCES

Baldwin, J. Giovanni's Room. Vintage, 2013.

Bowlby, J. A Secure Base: Parent-Child Attachment and Healthy Human Development. Basic, 1988.

Celani, D. P. A Fairbairnian Structural Analysis of the Narcissistic Personality Disorder. Psychoanalytic Review, 101 (3), June 2014.

Fonagy, P. Attachment Theory and Psychoanalysis. Other, 2001.

Goldstein, D. Two States. Eight Testbooks. Two American Stories. New York Times, 01-12-2020.

Harlow, H.F. Learning to Love. Jones and Bartlett, 1971.

Jones, E. The Life and Work of Sigmund Freud. Basic, 1961.

Riviera, E. P. The Linked Self in Psychoanalysis. (Eds.) R. Losso, L.S. DeSetton, and D. Sharff. Routledge, 2017.

Rothman, J. Same Difference: What the Idea of Equality can do for us, and what it can't. The New Yorker, 01-13-2020, pp. 26-3.

LILIES OF THE FIELD

> Consider the lilies of the field, how they
> grow; they toil not, neither do they spin.
>
> —Matthew 6:28

Many human affairs are characterized by a focus on what is other. We define ourselves in contrast to others who are different. Furthermore it is often the case that these others are seen by us as inferior. Though just who others are differs from case to case, the logic of us versus them is common.

Such a situation leads to alterity in which it is held people other than myself are different and inferior. President Trump (see Rohde, 2020) said to an audience of the Values Voter Summit:

> Extreme left-wing radicals, both inside and outside the government, are determined to shred our Constitution and eradicate the beliefs we all cherish. They are trying to hound you from the public square, and weaken the American family, and indoctrinate our children (p 32).

Based on the above description, Trump has divided the group of Americans into an us-group (actually a me-group) and a them-group. Secondly he has located all bad in the them-group. It would certainly be arguable that the things of which Trump accused the them-group are actually true of him. Thirdly he may be seen trying to institutionalize this view.

A similar example is when Attorney General Barr (Ibid) wrote:

> We live in an increasingly militant, secular age…As part of this philosophy, we see a growing hostility toward religion, particularly Catholicism…It is no accident that the homosexual movement, at one or two percent of the population,

gets treated with such solicitude, while
the Catholic population, which is over a
quarter of the country, is given the back
of the hand (p. 37).

Again, it is those-guys who are bad, even though it
strains credulity to imagine the gay-rights movement
is bullying the Catholic Church.

What is going on? Why do we need to construct an
"other?"

It was Klein (1932) who felt that, in the ordinary
course of events, an infant has both good and bad feelings. Klein felt the first move an infant makes is to
locate the bad elements outside itself. This leaves the
child with good elements and therefore okay. Klein
called this the "paranoid-schizoid position." Such a
maneuver allows the infant to feel he or she is good,
but, having located bad in the surround, the infant
must now fear the surround—as that is where the bad
stuff is.

Such a move, nonetheless, allows the infant to develop the beginnings of a positive sense of self-esteem. As the infant grows and develops more capacity
he or she can move beyond the external relocation
program and begin to realize there are bad elements in
the him or herself. This is what Klein called the "de-
pressive position." Such an infant is able to know he
or she has both good and bad elements as opposed to
being all good.

Fairbairn, a Scottish psychiatrist, worked with populations of young people who were the victims of trauma, including rape and other forms of severe abuse (see Mitchell and Black, 1995). Fairbairn posed the following question: What do you do if you are an infant, and the person upon whom you rely for survival is hurting you? Such a child is in an impossible position. If the child gives vent to the anger he or she feels, the child endangers his or her source of support. If the child loses support, the fear is he or she will die.

If, on the other hand, the child does not experience the anger he or she feels, the child does significant damage to his or her developing self. The idea Fairbairn developed in working with these young people was as follows: In order to preserve the attachment necessary for survival with the hurtful and abusive parent, the child splits off parts of the self and represses them. That is, the part of the self that is angry and the part of the self that desires a loving parent are both split off. These are then consigned to the unconscious.

Thus the child removes both love and hate from consciousness. Free of the need to respond to either, the child can tolerate a connection to the caregiver. It may be a dead sort of connection, but it *is* a connection.

Fairbairn also held there were internal relationships in the child that correspond to external relationships (object relations). That is, the part of the self that is angry has an internal target for that anger. This is an internalized representation of the hurtful parent. Fairbairn called this the *bad object* (the anti-libidinal object). The angry self (the anti-libidinal ego) directs its anger and hatred toward the bad object (the anti-libidinal object).

Similarly the desiring self (the libidinal ego) has an idea of a parent who would be good and kind to the child. This is the good object (the libidinal object). The desiring self longs to attain connection with the good object. All of this goes on unconsciously.

The idea here is that there is a part of the self that hates the parent for his/her abuse. There is also a part of the self that longs for a parent who would be able to deliver love. The part of the self that hates the parent also hates the part that desires the parent to become loving. Like the saga of Lucy and the football, seeking this kind of love never works out. Hurtful people do not become loving.

The critical element is this: *anything that can be associated with the bad object will be despised or opposed.* Anything that resembles the bad object will be responded to in the same way as the original bad object. If my hurtful mother was autocratic, I will hate autocracy. If my hurtful mother was phony, I will hate phoniness. If my hurtful mother was pious, I will hate piety. If my hurtful mother was in charge, I will hate those who are in charge.

This is how religious people can hate non-religious people. They are other. Non-religious people can hate religious people. Liberal people can hate conservative people. Conservative people can hate liberal people. Educated people can hate non-educated people, and non-educated people can hate the educated. The wealthy can hate the poor, and the poor can hate the wealthy. Anything I think is bad will be, unconsciously, bad in the same way the frustrating parent was bad.

That is pretty bad.

Soon everybody hates everybody. And all this hatred begins with the interaction between a hurt infant and his or her parent. The amount of hate depends on the *degree* of hurt. That is where I learned it. The one who doesn't get it right and is hurtful is my enemy. I desire what is possible with one who would please me. But, try as I may, such a person cannot be found.

What I *am* able to find is one who operates like the hurtful parent. This is a person who makes sense, who *feels right,* as such a person is a known type. Having found this person, I can begin the project of trying to turn them into one who would please me. It is a project that can be attempted over and over.

As long as one remains in the same milieu as his or her original family, this same pattern will appear sensible. This is how differing causes and cultural positions come to be emotionally loaded. The affection or hate I have for such affairs is of ancient origin. Unexamined, I can carry it through an entire life. The powerful emotions find representation, but they are poorly understood, if at all.

That is, I know I am strongly opposed to some position, but I don't know why this is the case. I may, for example, detest authorities, but I don't know from whence this comes. I think college students are communists, but I don't know why.

I may become caught up in a movement that consumes much or most of my time. I may campaign for or against abortion. I may campaign for or against military strength.

Alexander (2020) wrote:

> White nationalism has been emboldened by our president, who routinely unleashes hostile tirades against black and brown people — calling Mexican migrants criminals, "rapists" and "bad people," referring to developing African nations as "shithole countries" and smearing a district of the majority-black city of Baltimore as a "disgusting, rat and rodent infested mess." Millions of Americans are cheering, or at least tolerating, these racial hostilities.

This is how scapegoating is established. People of color become the carrier of the bad traits of White people. White people gave those traits to them. In this way White people don't need to notice the bad traits that are really their own. "White people" becomes a construction. It is that group that is good. "People of color" likewise becomes a construction. It is that group that is bad.

Such a program is a way in which White people can siphon off their aggression and legitimize it. Also, the category "White people" only exists in relation to the category of "people of color." It is assumed there is an ontological difference between them. Considerable energy is expended to maintain this split. If the split were to collapse, the dynamics of the psychology that maintains it would be exposed.

As our culture becomes more homogenous, such positions become harder to justify and maintain. Increasingly it is seen that *both* the us and them groups are distortions. These distortions become obvious with increased group exposure. Cut off and isolated groups are more able to maintain distortions of themselves and others, because they are less in contact with each other.

As the culture matures, homogenization increasingly occurs in large urban centers due to the fact more groups are represented there. Resistance to this is encountered in isolated or rural regions where multiple groups are less common. Soon there develops a difference between the outlook expressed by urban groups and that expressed by rural groups. Stemming from different needs, conflict ensues.

This is quite a lot of baggage for parent-infant interaction to carry.

It is at this point that concepts of power enter the picture. Love is accepting. Anger and hate are rejecting. In a general sense one's primary direction in life is either aimed toward acceptance of others, or it is aimed toward rejection of them. This is also true for the groups to which one belongs. And it definitely is true of the environment one provides for one's infant. Learning from me, the child will be guided toward acceptance as a rule or toward rejection. I may have racial, religious, and political rigidity, or I may not.

Survival of the individual as well as the group hinges on whether or not it can find a way to function as a somewhat coherent entity. This does not mean everyone must think the same thing (which is impossible) or behave in the same way. It means the group must find a way to *include* as many people as possible within the umbrella of the group—those we like and those we don't.

This was an ideal given lip service by the Christian church, though from the start it was poorly practiced. The reason for this is that, during the time of the codification of the faith, there were numerous gospels and tracts in existence. Church fathers saw the necessity of limiting the number of these writings that would be considered orthodox. Other writings were rejected and considered to be heresies. Only approved texts and practices were condoned (Hatch, 1957). There was thus a clear establishment of an us versus a them system.

The subsequent history of Christianity is replete with accounts of war and hatred between Christians and non-Christians (see Nixey, 2018). This continues today in the struggle between some American groups and Muslims.

All persons are affected by the need for the other. If nothing else, one can oneself attempt to avoid such a pattern. This requires keeping an open mind, as much as possible, and seeing opposing group from a more synoptic position which includes both sides. That is, such groups are part of a larger whole. This is not an impossible task. It does require one to accept his or her own shortcomings and flaws. The enemy we have been opposing is not entirely external.

Blumenthal (2020) wrote:

> Americans often explained their radicalized fears of indigenous people and Black Americans through paranoid conspiracies claiming these groups were not only outside of the American national family but also directed by external threats to the nation. Before the Civil War, they claimed indigenous people were directed by the British and that Haiti influenced slave revolts in the U.S. And they used those external conspiracies to justify internal repression.

It is hard to imagine this is what genuine inclusion looks like. Trump has simply expanded on this theme:

> Where Trump's War diverges from much of America's history of repression is where he situates its source. The subversive behavior he aims to repress does not emanate from indigenous people in the forest; it doesn't originate from the USSR; it isn't directed by the pope; there is no anti-American "axis of evil." The demons animating Trump's imagination are directed by the Democratic Party (Ibid).

Such comments echo views of Baldwin (1972, 1992) who remarked that those harmed by power are likely to lose allegiance to that power. When the number of these people becomes significant, they represent a group that cannot be controlled by those in power.

> ...no kingdom can maintain itself by force alone. Force does not work the way its advocates seem to think it does. It does not, for example, reveal to the victim the strength of his adversary. On the contrary, it reveals the weakness, even the panic of his adversary, and this revelation invests the victim with patience (1972, pp. 88-89).

Psychologically, power may be considered to be an admission of the failure of ingenuity. Students of behavior know that the arrangements of rewards and their absences are a far more effective means of eliciting desired behavior that is punishment.

Said Baldwin (Ibid):

> ...the Christian Church has betrayed and blasphemed and dishonored that Savior in whose name they have slaughtered millions and millions and millions of people. And if this mighty objection seems trivial, it can only be because of the total hardening of the heart and the coarsening of the conscious among those people who believed that their power has given them the exclusive right to history (p. 49).

Several of Baldwin's notions are picked up again by Coates (2015) who suggested the progress of people who believe they are White has been based on looting and violence (p. 6).

> Americans believe in the reality of "race" as a defined, indubitable feature of the natural world. Racism—the need to ascribe bone-deep features to people and then to humiliate, reduce, and destroy them—in-

evitably follows from this inalterable condition (p. 7).

In this way race can be thought of as a basic quality of nature instead of a construction involving status, power, and privilege.

An an expanded view of the history of human beings reveals these creatures evolved, over millions of years, from origins in Africa. All races developed from these origins. History also makes it clear how difficult it has been for human creatures to get along with each other. Groups have long sought domination over others and have defined differences in a multitude of ways.

In America the construction has prevailed that White people are naturally superior to people of color and therefore have the right to exploit and abuse people of color, thus establishing an economic system in which people of color are required to live in inferior ways. Importantly, such a construction is not universally held in the world.

...the law has become an excuse for stop-
ping and frisking you, which is to say, for
furthering the assault on your body. But a
society that protects some people through
a safety net of schools, government-
backed home loans, and ancestral wealth
but can only protect you with the club of
criminal justice has either failed at enforc-

ing its good intentions or has succeeded at something much darker (Coates, pp. 17, 18).

At Howard University, Coates discovered Black people from all over the world with their multiple personas able to interact in a world seemingly separate from the White world he was used to.

> "White America" is a syndicate arrayed to protect its exclusive power to dominate and control our bodies…the power of domination and exclusion is central to the belief in being white, and without it "white people" would cease to exist for want of reasons (p. 42).

It is important to analyze the psychology of White denial and the avoidance of the plight of people of color. Why conceive of the history of America in terms of White people only? Why construct a society that requires a permanent underclass? Why perpetuate this situation?

Why turn a blind eye to the practice of police in brutalizing and harassing this underclass? Why establish building codes that relegate people of color to defined and inferior areas where they are preyed upon and entrapped? Why maintain separate but unequal school systems, welfare systems, health care systems, financial systems, and employment systems?

Is White status worth that much?

It has been argued the election of Donald Trump was a direct reaction to the election of Barak Obama. The most fragile White people were deeply threatened by Obama's election and feared an erosion of their status and position. Trump was able to exploit these feelings as he opposed immigrants, especially immigrants of color, as well as honesty, integrity, and a grasp of the government he was leading.

Though it can be argued Trump is an extremely compromised person, whole sectors of the populous were enthralled by him and became reflexive supporters. These were people who had something to lose. No matter how minimal their situation was, they were at least better than people of color. And women. And LGBTQ persons. They were also better than foreigners, bi-costal elites, and students who study quantum mechanics and post-modern poetry.

They were especially superior to the godless heathens who were unswayed by fundamentalist religion and its demands for adherence. This included anyone opposed to White, male superiority and the demanded privilege of that group. The threatened group was serious. They were at the Alamo, and the battle was at hand.

What these White people demonstrated more than anything was how frightened they were. Besieged on every side, they were desperately mounting a defense. It was all they knew how to do. Their counter-attack was against change and the inevitable movement of growth. Fearing the loss of the life they had known; they were afraid of the future that would nevertheless engulf them.

The psychopathology of this position rests in its rigidity in the face of a fluid reality—as if being equal to my neighbor were a fate too terrible for me to bear. It is also a frightening display of the lack of empathy for one's fellow beings—simply on the basis of skin color or some other defining trait. As long as I can relax while the Latino man mows my lawn, Asian people do my laundry, Black people remove my garbage and service my car—as long as I feel a genuine sense of superiority to these people, the society remains off balance.

It is the criminal justice system that is called on to preserve this situation. Alexander (2020) wrote:

> Our nation's prison and jail population ha[s] quintupled in 30 years, leaving us with the highest incarceration rate in the world. A third of black men had felony records — due in large part to a racially biased, brutal drug war — and were relegated to a permanent second-class status. Tens of millions of people in the United

States had been stripped of basic civil and human rights, including the right to vote, the right to serve on juries and the right to be free of legal discrimination in employment, housing, education and basic public benefits.

Alexander argued there are "powerful racial dynamics and political forces" that made racial progress illusory (see also Davis, 1990, and Shakur, 2001). This was in part due to a failure to acknowledge our racist past. She suggested the election of Donald Trump with his embrace of White nationalism represented a "whiplash" to the election of Barak Obama. According to this view, the politics of Trumpism are not new. They are the same tactics that have been used over and over to preserve a racial hierarchy.

One thing that has changed is the animosity now directed toward immigrants, foreigners, and "illegals." Trump said:

> When Mexico sends its people, they're not sending their best...They're sending people that have lots of problems, and they're bringing those problems... They're bringing drugs. They're bringing crime. They're rapists.

Such views lead to action on the part of the criminal justice system as a means both of control and a shift of responsibility.

Coates wrote to his son:

> …the police departments of your country have been endowed with the authority to destroy your body. It does not matter if the destruction is the result of an unfortunate overreaction. It does not matter if it originates in a misunderstanding. It does not matter if the destruction springs from a foolish policy. Sell cigarettes without the proper authority and your body can be destroyed. Resent the people trying to entrap your body and it can be destroyed. Turn into a dark stairwell and your body can be destroyed. The destroyers will rarely be held accountable. Mostly they will receive pensions. And destruction is merely the superlative form of a dominion whose prerogatives include friskings, detainings, beatings, and humiliations (Ibid, p. 9).

The need to preserve the idea that American society is a White society is woven into history books presented to high school students (see Goldstein, 2020, Morrison, 2020). The need to create "others" upon whom we can project our own shortcomings and hostility has had a long and vigorous history. Everything would be fine if it weren't for "those" people.

> White nationalism, at its core, reflects a belief that our nation's problems would be solved if only people of color could somehow be gotten rid of, or at least better controlled. In short, mass incarceration and mass deportation have less to do with crime and immigration than the ways we've chosen to respond to those issues when black and brown people are framed as the problem (Alexander, Ibid).

The need for the "other" has been ubiquitous in human affairs. It has always been required of us to find persons to fill this category, or else we will have to understand that both good and bad impulses reside in ourselves. This would require us to bring previously split off parts of ourselves into consciousness. It would require a different understanding of what it is to be human.

When our training requires us to become partial-creatures, we lose sight of who we really are. In our rush to be both superior and innocent we must turn a blind eye to those who are neither—and ultimately to ourselves.

REFERENCES

Alexander, M. The Injustice Of This Moment Is Not An 'Aberration': From mass incarceration to mass deportation, our nation remains in deep denial. New York Times, 01-27-2020.

Baldwin, J. No Name on the Street. Dell, 1972.

Baldwin J. The Fire Next Time. Vintage, 1992.

Blumenthal, P. Donald Trump is Writing a Terrifying New Chapter in the History of Political Repression. Huffington Post, 08-01-2020.

Coates, T-N, Between the World and Me. Spiegel and Grau, 2015.

Davis, A. Women, Culture, and Politics, Vintage, 1990.

Goldstein, D. Two States. Eight Textbooks. Two American Stories. New York Times, 01-12-2020.

Hatch, E. The Influence of Greek Ideas on Christianity. Harper, 1957.

Klein, M. The Psychoanalysis of Children. Hogarth, 1932.

Mitchell, S. A., and Black, M.J. Freud and Beyond: A history of modern psychoanalytic thought. Basic, 1995.

Morrison, T. The Source of Self-Regard: Selected Essays, Speeches, and Meditations. Vintage International, 2020.

Nixey, C. The Darkening Age: The Christian destruction of the classical world. Houghton Mifflin, 2018.

Rohde, D. Sword and Shield: William Barr's mission to maximize executive power and protect Trump. The New Yorker, 01-20-2020, pp. 32-43.

Shakur, A. Assata: An Autobiography. Lawrence Hill Books, 2001.

LIVING IN WATER

> Here lies one whose name
> was writ in water
>
> — John Keats

I had a patient who was a professor of physics. He told me it is a consequence of the equations worked out by Einstein that there is no known place in the universe that is static. I thought: Einstein obviously had not encountered the human mind.

Everything around us changes. Yet so many of us are repelled by change. We want everything to stay the same.

It is easier that way. Freud recognized this as the death wish. We say: You aren't the way you used to be."

Clearly, adjusting to repeated change is more difficult as it requires constant effort. This is how we become dinosaurs. We stick with what is old—and familiar. Bowlby (1988) recognized that the familiar seems safe. It is, he said, how we are wired. He considered this to be the basis of attachment between an infant and his or her mother. And since humans are an alloplastic species (born helpless) an extended period of development is necessary.

No two infants have the same development experience. This is obvious, because no two infants have the same mother—even if they do. There are changes in the way the "same" mother will interact with two different infants. Attachment theorists (Bowlby, Ibid., Fonagy, 2001) have held that the important variable in mother-child interactions is that the mother needs to hold the infant in her mind. That is, the infant needs to find him or herself more or less accurately represented in the mind of the mother. This results in a mutual resonance which is the foundation of empathy.

The mother must be capable of reflective function which is the ability to think of the infant as having thoughts and feelings in the way she has. It is this that leads to the infant learning he or she is a person who matters. When reflective function is missing the mother relates to the infant's *exterior*. That is, the infants physical needs are attended to, but the human connection is missing. An even more extreme case results when neither the psychological nor physical dimensions are considered.

The logic involved here is that when the infant is able to develop a secure attachment as a result of the effective use of reflective function and reasonable attunement of the caretaker, that secure base is internalized and becomes the "ground" upon which the growing child stands in dealing with life. Such a child tends to feel more secure *no matter what he or she does.*

In contrast, the child who is insecurely attached due to various empathic failures on the part of his or her caretaker isn't so sure he or she is okay. Such a child may regard the world as dangerous, chaotic, or inconsistent. Such a child is far less confident than his or her securely attached peer.

In American culture there is a difference between strict father families and nurturing parent families (Lakoff, 2016). Essentially strict father families require members to obey rules and comply with parent demands. Nurturing parent families are interested in how each member feels. Such a difference leads to adults who are primarily concerned with law and order as opposed to adults who are primarily interested in having each person's feelings matter.

Though it is certainly possible that empathy may be found in strict father families as well as a lack of empathy found in nurturing parent families, these outcomes would seem to go against the grain of such orientations.

These notions in general concern the development of individuals who are more or less able to cope with change. They also speak to the recent polarity in American culture. Adjusting to rapidly changing aspects of technology and information requires resources that obeying rigid principles lack. The demand is on *constant* and *rapid* change. And as time goes on, it is speeding up.

In some fields information learned during a college education is practically obsolete by the time students graduate. For many pursuits learning is a life-long enterprise as new developments eclipse current principles. A complex trade-off ensues in which developed experience interweaves with new developments. The requirement for updating is constant.

The speed of cultural development routinely pits children against their parents and their parents against them. No longer can one assume one's child will have a similar experience to what the parent had in school and the world. A result of this is a reality that has become highly individualistic.

Anais Nin wrote: "We don't see things as they are; we see things as we are." That is we see things from where we stand. And where we stand is a unique position. It is easy to elide or erase such differences, especially when they involve intersectional elements—as is common. In light of this, a humane society must be seen in terms of inclusion. Like the nurturing parent family, everyone's feelings get to count.

Cultural polarity, by contrast, seeks to *exclude.* It seeks to valorize one group over another. May the best side win.

Polarity and exclusion thrive where empathy fails or is for some reason inappropriate. The ultimate breakdown of humanity is war, where instead of trying to understand each other, we try to destroy each other. The innate capacity to destroy lies in opposition to the survival of a humane world.

A significant problem is that typically one can only be as empathic as his or her environment has allowed. Considerate parents who listen are very different from angry parents who punish. Society advances as it is able to move from the latter to the former.

So how is that even possible? Millions of people live moment to moment in a climate of fear and exclusion. Millions are affected by medical issues they neither understand nor know how to treat. Millions of children are beaten, berated, excluded, ignored, starved, scapegoated, gaslighted, and left with no one who can hear them. The obvious answer is *someone* must hear them. *Someone* must try to improve their plight. Someone must be dedicated to help the culture become more fluid, more flexible, more changing.

Success in this endeavor is always incremental and is subject to the prevailing currents of the time. Human history is filled with those who help humanity advance as well as those who stand in the way of this project. Still, each person who works to understand him or herself improves the lot of the whole. Every street that has a healthy person living on it is blessed.

II

Change radiates in a different direction. Everything that is alive changes. Organisms mature, learn, develop, and are forced to cope with constantly shifting circumstances. Nothing remains the same for long (death? taxes?). Everything that is alive is in a kind of motion.

This is a kind of change that demands attention even if we have avoided respecting other changes. Human beings have a finite term of life, and that time is always on the move.

There is no going back—even if one tries to go back. What is past is past. This goes for events and also for one's time of living. And as it goes, it seems to speed up. When one is a child, summers (the good time) seemed almost endless. When we are older, they seem less than a month. The hours one has are priceless, but they cannot ever be held. Like a night train rushing to its destination, we flash past the accomplishments of our lives.

Soon it seems everything is evaporating. As one ages there is less and less that can be held. Things come into our lives and go out at astonishing speed. We no sooner get used to something than it is gone. It comes to us this is also true for our lives. We will not be able to retain anything, no possessions, no acquaintances, no experiences, nothing.

This is to be living in water. It is the realization as one brushes one's hand across a loved one's shoulder that it may be the last time—as surely the last time is coming. One walks amid water, and the water swirls and changes. This requires an ability to let go. Why is that so hard?

In our culture we acquire things. We define ourselves by them. Yet we cannot hold onto them. I read about a woman in Texas who was buried in her Ferrari. I wonder how that went for her? We define ourselves by our social positions, but we can't hold onto these either. We are daily walking through a disappearing world.

The progress of life involves a gradual giving up of control. As one's life lengthens, change occurs more rapidly. There is nothing to grasp—it is all water. One walks through one's rooms. They stand with their carefully collected junk. It is yours, but not really, is it? One starts one's car for a drive. Yours? Ha. The leaves fill out on the trees and then drop. Cold weather comes and goes. One's children are young and at home and then they are not. People one knows veer off in different directions. Nothing stays still.

It is remarkable how all of our acquisitions eventually come to nothing. Possessions, knowledge, awareness, passions, openings are all like apples: they grow, become ripe, and then wither away.

III

Equated to life's motions are the identities we have. If
we continue to grow, our identities are changing all the
time. Who we are today is not who we were yesterday, a
decade ago, last year. Soon we are so little like our
young selves, we wonder who we are.

There are milestones. Becoming a teenager changes
one as does going to college, becoming a parent, world
travel, aging, and experiencing different contexts. This is
not to mention tragedy, failure, and becoming more real.
There is so much to learn from disaster, how it feels, how
it tears down, how it sobers, how it reorients.

Kohut (1984) felt the thing about which we are most in
denial is reality. He knew how difficult it is to be able to
shed one's distortions and face reality honestly.   It
shouldn't be so surprising this requires endless struggle.
Reality is too harsh for many, if not most, of us. Among
its other attributes it is simply brutal. Things are what
they are and nothing else. One is who one is, no matter
how one regards oneself.

I have always found it helpful to think of life as a series
of chapters. There is the childhood chapter, school chapter, young adult chapter, &c. Each of these chapters has a
beginning and an end. I have always had difficulty with
transitions. When chapters are coming to an end, I don't
want them to stop. I want to include more in them. Then
the next chapter inexorably begins, and life seems better.

Growing means change. It also means uncertainty, which is difficult to manage. It means letting go of how things have been and a willingness to embrace the unknown. This can happen on a simple trip or when one changes arrangements in one's life.

None of it is easy. Even standing still is not easy as everything around one is changing. The world one knew has disappeared. Life itself is intertwined with this constant change. Living in its essence involves change. But that is not how we think of it. We think it is constant. What we achieve today will still be valid tomorrow. We have been taught to think in terms of permanence. And because of this, we think change is problematic.

As the blinders are slowly removed from one's eyes by effort and study, one discovers the world is not the place one thought it was, and the self is not who one thought it was. It is as if one has been living a meta-life, a chimera induced by the fog of one's experience to keep one from grasping a better truth.

And then one is always starting again. It is a new world and a new self, and a new way of being has to be found. Such points are always bittersweet as they involve sadness at the artifice one has maintained while at the same time they offer the possibility of the future.

Where one lives is different, who one knows is different, what one understands is different. There is no going back. Once tasted, this new awareness must be dealt with, and hopefully in a way that facilitates further transitions.

Perhaps who we really are will never be known by us. Perhaps it won't be known by those around us. The world of seeing is always creating itself and expanding. One has never gone far enough. The stages of ourselves as the stages of our lives correspond to the chapters we have lived.

Then one day, in the afternoon, it stops. We have no more tomorrows, no more growing. No time to write another note, read another article, or experience anything else.

And after us, it begins again.

IV

As life approximates water all things become more transient. There is no place one can call one's own. One is but a temporary inhabitant. In this space one does what he or she feels is essential—what he or she alone could do.

The streets one has grown used to seem to exist for an odd sort of transient thing. One sees the people along them dying off. Sunsets have always been there, but now one's time with them is limited. Seasons slip away too quickly.

It is disorienting. Before one has counted on a kind of stability. School had its structure. One's work life had its structure. The years one lived had their structure. But now there seems to be no structure, no exoskeleton. Upon what can one rely? How to find meaning in such a life?

The answer is the same as it has always been. One's answer is to ground oneself in the truths of one's identity. One reason this is so hard to do is that one's identity is a limited thing. There are clearly things one is not. Before in one's life there was always time to pick up another skill, take another trip, polish another ability. One could rely on vast resources beyond oneself. The resources provided part of the meaning.

Now it is different. One is less widely plugged in. Younger voices are filling the halls where one used to walk. They are the carriers of new ideas, available to them, because they are not cluttered with the worn-out notions we acquired. What is important in their time is different. Society, as well as the intellectual arena, is now a different place. We discover we are dated.

We thought it would go on forever, we who so often sold our visions for a song. After flowering, the rose does not return to the status of a bud. It grows shabby and then falls apart. It is a painful metaphor for those of us now counting the days.

We realize at once our lives are like a journey of a ship. (I think of Thomas Cole's paintings in the National Gallery.) Our ship sets out, we have great dreams—almost all of which are fantasies, we run into the harsh realities of existence, we try to find a way to survive, and then we emerge into a bizarre sort of calm.

Finding a center in calm is a new task, one for which we were not trained—being raised in clamor. This is a task for those who are looking at the twilight of their productive years and who want to start over, want to use their hard-won awareness to create something that matters.

It is the wrong wish. The greatest masters did not live this way. They found what was significant in themselves, in the strange combination they were, to articulate that nature clearly. Every nature truly expressed makes us richer, makes the world more complete. Our task in the calm is difficult, because it requires us, as perhaps never before, to confront our own limitations and potentials.

It is with this collection of junk we now must create.

We must bring our voyage home with honor. Though we cannot retain anything, we can find ways to make our journey matter. We can exalt in the water as long as we can. Water is now our medium. It allows us what we need. Living in water is different from living in structure, but it is no less vital. It is just different.

One summer I visited the little medieval chateau above the Swiss town of Muzot where the poet Rilke had written the *Sonnets to Orpheus* and finished the *Duino Elegies*. It was a beautiful day in the Alps. Someone with an Audi was living there then. I stood in the field by the

chateau a long time trying to imagine Rilke being there.
Alive. Driven.

The space was sacred to me, because I had read Rilke
so much. I could imagine him standing on the little bal-
cony out back of the chateau. But he wasn't there. It was
simply a place where he once had been. He had become
part of the water upon which I sailed.

REFERENCES

Bowlby, J. A Secure Base: Parent-Child Attachment and Healthy Human Development. Basic, 1988.

Fonagy, P. Attachment Theory and Psychoanalysis. Other, 2001.

Kohut, H. How does Psychoanalysis Cure? Chicago, 1984.

Lakoff, G. The Political Mind: A Cognitive Scientist's Guide to Your Brain and its Politics. Penguin. 2009.

Lakoff, G. Moral Politics: How Liberals and Conservatives Think. Third Edition. Chicago, 2016.

AMERICAN DARKNESS

The proverbial dumb-ass who lives across the tracks on the other side of town didn't choose to be born there. He or she didn't choose to have abusive parents, uneducated friends, pervasive drug and alcohol abuse, and a complicated psychological profile.

There were reasons during the run-up to the Trump presidency approximately forty percent of Americans were angry, resentful, restive, and miserable. They had been cut out. Business elites had cut them loose. Reasoning that the only thing that matters is bottom-line net profit for shareholders, almost half of Americans suddenly found themselves unable to make an adequate living.

Poverty rates skyrocketed, as did drug abuse. Properties were lost as were resources for health care, and there were no jobs anywhere. Often, there wasn't enough to eat, and school tuition was but a dream. These people were angry.

It was this group Donald Trump and his election efforts sought to exploit. Trump, used to being an aggrieved outsider, understood the game cold. He knew about the rage. He knew about the unfairness. He spoke this language eloquently.

Democrats, locked into establishment connections, did not think the left out, angry people had a case—so the Democrats ignored them in favor of supporting the establishment class that had destroyed the lives of so many for profit.

Hillary Clinton displayed little or no empathy for this suffering group. She coldly called them "deplorables." Her people were the oppressors. They were so entitled in their outlook, they neglected to check the rear door—where the hurt and voiceless people could sneak in. And sneak in is just what they did.

The people from the other side of the track won the election, and the Trump years were born.

This is something for Americans to contemplate. It is not a game of the-best-man-wins. It is a challenge to a country that needs to find a way to include all of its people.

America is challenged to become, not the best-and-the-brightest, but the nation of all-the-people.

II

Trump was a person of grievance. Badly mistreated as a child by a combative, arrogant father and a vain, self-centered mother, Trump was early on a problem (Frank, 2018). He threw things over the fence at the neighbor's baby in its crib. He surreptitiously amassed a collection of switchblades and knives. He was a bully at school and constantly in trouble at home. He was eventually sent to a military school to reform him. He immediately became a big-shot in the peer group at the military school and strengthened himself into a person of power.

In short, Trump resembled the most disturbed of the kids from across the track except that his family had means.

Still, the bully, the argumentative big-shot, the manipulator of outcomes, remained. Trump followed his father into New York real estate where he made and lost fortunes. Never disciplined, Trump relied on his gut-instincts. Unburdened by a sense of empathy, he took advantage of everything he could. He loved to show off. He was made for TV, and his show was a success.

Trump was a con who lived by his wits. Such types are well known in the business community. Always flashy, always in the spotlight, always spinning a story that was as spectacular as it was flimsy. His women were beauty queens. He dined at the best places. Manipulative business deals made him into a billionaire. He lived in opulence on Fifty Avenue in New York City—downtown. He flew in his own plane and helicopter. Mr. Big.

Trump was so skilled at the fine art of salesmanship and bullshit, no one could lay a hand on him. He could make up any answer—and evade the rest. He rarely played by the rules. It was his way, and it worked. It did, however, leave considerable wreckage behind him, which he ignored.

This is the picture of a person who could never belong to the system. The system was his to con. Instead of living by the rules, Trump learned to live by his wits. He was the kid in class just waiting for the moment he could foment chaos. Having one foot in the gutter, he clearly saw the dark side of American society. He saw the poverty, the sickness, the substance abuse, the rage, and the grievance. His contenders in the presidential race were from the establishment. They did not see what Trump saw.

And he rode this awareness to success. Just barely.

Stunned by his election, the establishment tried to make sense of it. They tried thinking in political terms to little avail. They tried thinking in business terms to no avail. They were captive to their own lens and knew little about those who resent the system.

Meanwhile, Trump began to govern the way he did everything else. He sought power to benefit himself. In a large sense, the system of government was not his friend. He was a power unto himself. He did not seek to learn about the system of government. He did not seek to learn about the law. He had no interest in foreign relations.

Instead, he sought to implement the world-according-to-Trump. It was this world, not the United States government, that interested him.   His views prevailed. Authorities and experts were a problem as they were attuned to the wrong thing: the political establishment. Trump began replacing them with his own people, who may not know anything about the tasks they were given, but they were unwavering in their loyalty to Trump. Many agencies were gutted, and others were left dysfunctional. The structures of government did not know how to deal with this man who ignored them and destroyed their credibility.

No friend of the legal system—or of any form of laws or constraints—Trump took them over at the start. Trump, uninterested in justice, was interested in the survival of the world-according-to-Trump. He did what he could to cripple the legal system or to pack it with people sympathetic to his cause.

The people who had elected him were especially upset by the progress Black people had made in U.S. society. They despised President Obama. They essentially longed for the Fifties, which they took to be America's golden era. The world since then had seen too many changes, all of which took the culture away from this Fifties ideal. Religious attendance had plummeted. Sexual morality had changed. The bottom had fallen out of the economy for working people. And views of people of color were changing.

Always able to think of themselves a cut above people of color, such thoughts were now becoming less possible for uneducated White people. This created an enormous threat. These uneducated White males didn't want to be the bottom rung on the ladder. White supremacist groups became more popular. These were groups that collected grievance and hatred. This was funneled into an effort to bring back the outlook that prevailed in the Fifties. Then, Blacks were inferior to Whites. Gay and transgendered people were ostracized. There was a good living to be made in blue collar pursuits. People were again faithful to (evangelical concepts of) god.

Trump became their champion. He did not oppose them as the establishment did. These White males mobbed Trump's political rallies. They wore his paraphernalia. They roared approval at his open hostility to the establishment.

After Trump was elected and it was clear he had vanquished his rivals, Republicans throughout the government began to swing behind Trump and support him. This required a fair reach. Trump held few Republican views. He was not interested in supporting the Republican party but was interested in having the Republican party support him.

When Trump was elected, the Republicans had been out of office for eight years. They were the outsiders who were campaigning against the establishment and the establishment's candidate, Hillary Clinton. The fit with Trump was made in heaven. Trump was the original outsider. He wanted to take over the government, not for the Republicans, but for himself. But he ran on the Republican ticket. Republicans therefore welcomed him as one of them.

They supported him enthusiastically. He had vanquished the foe. He had brought victory to "our side." Slowly but steadily, the Republican party became the party of Trump. They supported his views and positions. They looked the other way at his antics and outrages. They covered up for him. And in one giant gesture, they failed to impeach him when he was obviously at fault.

They handed him the whole platter and with it, what remained of their honor. This phenomenon, of people willing to accommodate and support corrupt regimes, has a long history. Hoffmann (1974) sought to make classifications of such people. He noticed that, whatever their background, these people felt their personal situations would be improved by aligning with the occupiers.

Applebaum (2020) drew parallels between the Trump phenomenon and events involving Vichy France, East German fascists, and Communists. In each of these areas people were coerced to accept "an alien ideology or a set of values that [were] in sharp conflict with their own." In each case, the change was not foisted on people all at once, but gradually, in a series of small steps—changes that could be accommodated.

It is a game we each learn throughout our lives. We don't tell our parents they are wrong, because they would flip out. We don't tell the teacher he or she is boring, because it would not go well for us. We don't tell the professor he or she is biased and narrow-minded, because he or she would retaliate. We don't tell the boss he or she is a tyrant, because we would get fired. We learn, in short, never to speak the truth. This allows us to stay within the group instead of being cast out of the group. It is the group's price. The toadies who swung their support behind the president were no different.

Trump began by lying about the size of the crowd at his inauguration. He compelled the National Parks Service to produce altered photographs of this event. In his inaugural address he claimed the U.S. government was an establishment that had profited at the expense of the people—even though the government had been democratically elected according to the Constitution.

The "replacement" of facts with Trump's "alternative facts" continued in a steady stream. Once supporters had overlooked the first few, it was easier to embrace those that followed.

Applebaum (Ibid) said:

> ...he has built a Cabinet and an administration that serve neither the public nor his voters but rather his own psychological needs and the interests of his own friends on Wall Street and in business and, of course, his own family.

Trump did not operate within the structure of the U.S. government as laid out in the Constitution. Trump operated in his own way within the sphere of his own personal project: the maintenance and survival of the power of Donald Trump.

The Republican party essentially collaborated in this project. In doing so, two things happened. The first was the party stopped being the known Republican party and became the Party of Trump. The second was that the notions of American democracy were attacked head on. Democratic rule requires people with differing views to debate these views and eventually come to an acceptable solution. This was the way the U.S. government operated, more or less, throughout its long history.

The Republicans began to refuse to play. They demanded things go their way or else. They refused to cooperate with anything other than what they wanted. This is the way, not of democracy, but totalitarianism. Those in power are able to determine the outcome and ignore other voices.

So why did the Republicans go along with this scheme. Applebaum gives several reasons:

> We can use this moment to achieve great
> things.
> We can protect the country from the president.
> I, personally, will benefit.
> I must remain close to power.
> LOL nothing matters.
> My side might be flawed, but the political
> opposition is much worse.

I am afraid to speak out.

The country was left in the hands of a president who didn't understand the government and had no desire to learn about it. American foreign relations were a shambles as was international trade. Attacks on minorities, people of color, LGBTQ people, and immigrants all escalated. The military was favored over education, health care, and social services. Police departments received surplus war machinery.

A poll taken by the National Opinion Research Center (NORC) at this time reported that only fourteen percent of American adults reported being very happy (Coleman, 2020). Only forty two percent felt the standard of living would improve for their children.

Then, into this climate, came the coronavirus, a deadly disease with no treatment, vaccine, or cure. Already devastating in China, Iran, and Italy, America had some time to get ready. Trump saw it as a threat to his reelection chances and minimized it. The epidemic became a pandemic. Soon thousands of Americans were dying or were being treated in overcrowded hospitals. Something had to be done. Health officials urged personal isolation, the wearing of masks, and avoidance of group interactions. Businesses, schools, churches, bars, and restaurants closed. The country went into lock-down.

Trump claimed it would quickly pass, and everything could get back to normal. Instead of quickly passing, the pandemic only got worse. Soon America had the worst record of managing the virus in the world. It had the most cases and the most deaths. There was no coherent strategy to cope with it. Trump accused mask-wearers of wearing masks to mock him. It was, of course, about him.

In the middle of this pandemic, George Floyd (see Chapter Three) was killed in Minneapolis. Race riots erupted nation-wide. This time, these riots were different. Large numbers of White people could see the problem and joined with Blacks to urge police reform. The long history of using the police departments to reinforce racism reached a turning point. Change was demanded.

America saw its dark hour.

With more people out of work at any time since the great depression, the economy in shambles, racism exposed in all its ugliness and cruelty—including the fact the coronavirus disproportionally attacked people of color, thousands upon thousands of Americans dead or seriously ill, schools closed, businesses closed, and fear everywhere—the government was essentially missing or useless to help.

Trump and his minions had nothing upon which to fall back. The tools of race-bating, health care attacking, opposition to international cooperation, and rants against scientists, intellectuals, and people who were informed had little support. American people wanted sensible policies, organized action, empathy, and concern for their well-being. Trump could provide none of these. His arsenal consisted of battle, resistance, obstruction, self-interest, pseudo-toughness, and cruelty.

The people who had wanted to return America to the atmosphere of the Fifties had instead delivered her to the gates of hell.

III

In the language of psychotherapy, Donald Trump may be thought of as a symptom. A symptom is a manifestation of a disorder. What is it about our culture than enabled Donald Trump to be elected?

Trump was born June 14, 1946 in Queens, New York. He grew up in Queens and attended Fordham University and (after cheating on the entrance exam) the University of Pennsylvania, from which he graduated with a bachelor's degree in economics. Trump's father owned a real estate management company, and his mother was a prominent socialite in Queens.

Trump was born at a time in American history when the country had endured a crushing economic depression and had been involved in two major world wars. Trump's childhood occurred at a time the country was getting back on its feet. A period of relative ease and calm occurred during the Fifties, during which working class families were able to flourish.

It must be said the relative ease and calm of the Fifties was primarily enjoyed by White males. Blacks and other people of color were treated abysmally. LGBTQ people were hounded, shamed, and jailed. Women were regarded as servants. Children were told to shut up and obey. Religions demonized non-followers. Authoritarianism was common.

The relative calm and ease of White men was shattered by the Sixties with conflicting views about the war in Viet Nam. American culture essentially split in two. On one side were those who wanted to return to the atmosphere of the Fifties and continue the development that had begun there. The other side wanted to upturn this pattern and create a new kind of society in which individual voices, regardless of how disruptive they were, could flourish.

The split was intense and deep. One group felt their way of life was being threatened and wanted to drive the disrupters out. The culture where fathers worked, mothers took care of the house and the family, and where children were groomed to be upstanding and contributing members of the society was, they held, the ideal. Especially difficult for this group to tolerate was the so called sexual revolution which took place following the wide-spread availability of oral contraception. This was seen as an assault on traditional morality.

The other side wanted none of this. Seeing the bucolic Fifties as a society of repression and artificiality, this group sought freedom from authoritarian dictates of the Fifties-type of culture and demanded an equal voice. Mass protests were held against corporate greed, repression of Black people, the army-industrial complex, an often autocratically applied legal system, and sexual conformity. In essence this was a conflict between tradition and invention.

The main centers of the forward-looking movement were in large urban areas. The traditionalists were located more frequently in the suburbs and in rural areas.   The lines hardened. Families were torn apart as the Woodstock generation opened a widely supported new way to be.

An area where a good deal of conflict occurred concerned religion.   In America, religion has always been a many-hued affair, ranging from strict-fundamentalist views all the way to nuanced and deeply-felt spirituality.   In short, the same conservative-liberal split occurs in religion that occurs in the society. It was the sexual-revolution, more than anything else, that rose the ire of the conservatives. Flatly against developing trends, this group opposed LGBTQ issues, casual sex, the hook-up culture, the late-night bar scene, and especially contraception and abortion.

Also, at this time, the restructuring of business and manufacturing by corporate elites began to eliminate blue color jobs. Many jobs were outsourced to overseas operations, and many were being replaced by robots and computers. The woes of the working class multiplied. There was an increasing gap between the social and economic life of college graduates and non-college types. Advanced degrees were becoming more common.

Education brought options unavailable to those without it. A new economic era was at hand which required education and flexibility. The conservative groups were being left behind.

The election of Barack Obama was "a pivotal moment in American history for many reasons including how it further inflamed the right wing of the Republican Party (Wilentz, 2019)." By Obama's time the Republican party had become:

> ...an "insurgent outlier in American politics: ideologically extreme...scornful of compromise; unpersuaded by convention, understanding of fact, evidence and science; and dismissive of the legitimacy of its political opposition (see Mann and Ornstein, 2016).

In short, the GOP establishment had abandoned normal party politics in favor of a "relentless polarization." They were determined to obstruct and oppose President Obama every step of the way. In doing so, they gave up the Republican Party's professed principles: free trade, small government, and fiscal responsibility. They dissevered themselves from democratic principles (see also Lakoff, 2016) .

In the run-up to the Trump election, the Democrats were little better. Caught in a split between corporate and establishment power versus politics of the people, Democrats chose power, thus abandoning the people who needed them. This left the poor and disenfranchised people to listen to Trump's promises.

Stenner (2020) made a distinction between conservatives and authoritarians.

It's really critical to help people understand the difference between conservatives and authoritarians. Conservatives are by nature opposed to change and novelty, whereas authoritarians are averse to diversity and complexity. It's a subtle but absolutely critical distinction.

Authoritarianism is a functional disposition concerned with maximizing "oneness" and "sameness" especially in conditions where the things that make us one and the same — common authority, and shared values — appear to be under threat.

…the whole of liberal democracy is in grave danger at this moment. But the fault lies with authoritarians on both the right and the left, and the solution is in the hands of non-authoritarians on both sides (see Edsall, 2020).

Wilentz (Ibid) contends that the Trump administration has extended efforts begun during the Bush administration, including alternate facts, gross falsehoods, huge financial benefits to corporations, severity toward immigrants, and relentless division of the electorate into warring camps.

So, to whom was all this double-talk, outright falsehood, and divisive resentment focused? Who was the audience?

It was the people who had been excluded, passed by, and thrown away. It was the poor people who had unwittingly paid for brokers' Ferraris. It was the American people who had led good lives though they didn't own a house on the hill. It was the people who had never read Ulysses and couldn't pick out a Rothko on the wall. These were the people whose kids didn't attend a university, have a secure job or funds to paint the house.

These were the people who were angry. Who wanted a break. Who wanted to feel some dignity and worth. These were the people who did boilermakers after work and who clipped coupons for the grocery store. Who drank beer and ate bratwursts with their friends on the Fourth of July. These were, in short, American citizens. They paid their taxes and obeyed the laws. They helped their children with their homework and consoled them when their love lives didn't work.

Opposed to these people were the extremely wealthy and corporate managers. Interested in maximizing profits and minimizing taxes, these groups lobbied governments heavily for advantageous treatment. And, since they had more clout, they routinely prevailed over the working class and the poor.

But there were others. There were those with more significant psychological problems.

It is important that the establishment, the police, and the political system has not been able to be compassionate and offer an olive branch to those who are hurt. This fact betrays the bankruptcy of the haves. With nothing they can give, the haves equate themselves with the have-nots. There is no moral superiority here. The good guys have nothing to give. How, then, are they the good guys?

When everyone is a taker, humanity dies.

It is hard to escape the notion the American ethos has devolved into a land of takers without a working sense of empathy. The Editorial Board of the New York Times (2020) argued:

> Over the past four decades, American workers have suffered a devastating loss of economic power, manifest in their wages, benefits and working conditions. The annual economic output of the United States has almost tripled, but, with the help of policymakers from both political parties, the wealthy hoarded the fruits.

The Editorial Board (Ibid) pointed out "The annual sum that has shifted from workers to owners now tops $1 trillion." The destruction of labor unions, and with them the voice of the people they represent, played a large part in this shift.

It is also hard to escape the psychological ramifications of such events. The people who support President Trump have been motivated to do so by experiences they have had and the lives they have lived. It is certainly not implausible to think these people have come from homes in which authoritarian attitudes were present along with a lack of empathy. In such environments it is often everyone-for-him or herself.

Such a situation is characterized in Moral Foundations Theory (Graham, Haidt, Koleva, Motyl, Iyer, Wojcik, and Ditto, 1992). These authors found:

> Liberals valued Care and Fairness more than did conservatives, whereas conservatives valued Loyalty, Authority and Sanctity more than did liberals.

Such views reflect quite different childhood training.

West (2017) called authority people "other-blamers." Such people have low self-worth and develop poor shame-tolerance in childhood. They develop ways to avoid or forestall shaming experiences. West said:

> Poor shame tolerance causes behaviors… including vindictive anger, lack of insight and accountability, dishonesty, impulsivity, entitlement, paranoia, lack of remorse and empathy, self-importance, and attention-seeking…They rarely admit feelings of inadequacy because they believe this would make them vulnerable to the same abuse and control they are perpetrating.

The childhoods of these people routinely include developmental or attachment trauma, "such as abusive, shaming, rejecting, or neglectful parenting." This certainly was the case in the childhood of Trump. Feeling unloved, unprotected, and inadequate, these children have difficulty developing empathy. Fear is a constant companion. Accepting accountability is avoided as is the idea that societal or relational norms apply to them. Disrespect and disregard of the law has been a hallmark of the Trump approach.

As Trump cares more about managing his fragile personality than he does about the well-being of the country, so Trump supporters also disregard concern for the country. It is about them and their "side." Ignoring others is made easier by depersonalizing them (alterity). It is this process of objectification of others that allows disregard and cruelty to increase over time.

West (Ibid) said:

> Because the Other-blamer refuses to compromise or engage in fair play, it becomes "every man for himself." Family members resent having to always give so the Other-blamer can take. They resent the Other-blamer lying and refusing to agree on facts. They resent always being blamed while the Other-blamer can never admit fault. Abuse victims often experience frustration because when they try to get through to the abuser, the rules of fair plan do not apply.

If I have experienced this pattern in childhood, I have no model for interpersonal reciprocity and caring. This will be my notion of how life is. I will bring it into my business dealings, my political activity, my relationships, and my parenting. The cycle will pass along.

I will resent my parents and, through them, the system. I will be in opposition to these figures and want to avenge the humiliations (narcissistic wounds) I feel I, and my like-minded group, have suffered at their hands. We will be enemies. *They* will display the disowned and devalued parts of myself which I have projected onto them. This, in turn, justifies my anger.

A country whose citizens do not care about each other resembles a troubled family. A country of warring polarities does this too. The American focus on wealth and power has damaged a focus on mutual well-being. The Trump years were the culmination of this pattern. Trump betrayed little interest in the good of the country. He was interested in the good of himself. His supporters battled an opposition that seemed scarcely human. Those with wealth and power mercilessly exploited everyone else.

The police force representing those with wealth and power murdered Black citizens. The coronavirus killed tens of thousands while the President did nothing and pretended it would all go away. Almost half the population was out of work. The U.S. Congress was deadlocked into polarity and accomplished next to nothing. Military spending increased while funds for education, health care, and social services languished.

These were the fruits of the drive for wealth and power.

Clearly a different path was required, one based on reason and interpersonal caring. It does not require a utopia. It simply requires concern for those without money and power. It requires a healing. It requires parents to genuinely care about how their children think and feel instead of correcting them to the parental view. It requires management to rearrange the profit system so all people are treated fairly.   It requires us to respect all people, regardless of their skin color, sexual orientation, or deformity, as human beings who matter.

In short, it requires a shift to an ethic of inclusion.

One of the oldest symbols is that of the cup. The purpose of the cup is to contain that which is poured into it. An adequate container is one that is able to contain all of what is poured into it. We, as Americans, must reconsider our role as containers—of our children, of each other, of those like us as well as those unlike us. All must be made to feel welcome.

Social rejection or exclusion must be seen as damaging. A rearrangement of the system of wealth is long overdue. A new approach will be carried forward by people who refuse to align themselves with the present structure. It is with them that America will begin its climb to the light.

REFERENCES

Applebaum, A. History will Judge the Complicit. The Atlantic, 7-8-2020.

Coleman, J. Americans at unhappiest level in almost 50 years, research finds. The Hill, 06-16-2020.

Edsall, T.B. The Whole of Liberal Democracy is in Danger at this Moment. New York Times, 07-22-2020.

Frank, J. A. Trump on the Couch: Inside the Mind of the President. Avery, 2018.

Graham, J., Haidt, J., Koleva, S., Motyl, M., Iyer, R., Wojcik, S. P., and Dirtto, P.H. Moral Foundations Theory: The Pragmatic Value of Moral Pluralism. Advances in Experimental Social Psychology, Vol. 47, Academic Press, 2013, pp. 55-130.

Hoffmann, S. Decline or Renewal? France since the 1930's. Viking, 1974.

Lakoff, G. Understanding Trump. RSN, 08-15-16.

Mann, T. E., and Ornstein, N. J. It's Even Worse Than It Looks: How the American Constitutional System Collided with the New Politics of Extremism. Basic, 2016.

Stenner, K. The Authoritarian Dynamic. Cambridge, 2005.

The Editorial Board. The Jobs we Need. New York Times, 06-24-2020.

West, H. In Relationship with an Abusive President. In The Dangerous Case of Donald Trump, (Ed.) B.X. Lee, St. Martin's, 2017.

Wilentz, S. The Culmination of Republican Decay. The New York Review of Books, 10-10-2019.

ASYMMETRY AND DOMINATION

Benjamin (1988) made a significant contribution to the psychoanalytic understanding of equality. Speaking from an interpersonal perspective, she stressed the notion of mutual interpersonal communion or empathic attunement. Such an experience, she argued, is that of two subjects being in profound connection. Her word for this was *resonance*.

Such a state is to be found in an ideal mother-infant connection. It requires the mother to seek recognition from the infant she realizes is another being. The infant, in turn, seeks recognition that the mother has indeed recognized the infant. Despite the differential between them, both parties must in this sense be considered equals by each other. Benjamin said there is "a necessary tension between self-assertion and mutual recognition that allows the self and other to meet as sovereign equals."

One may think of this kind of interaction as symmetrical. The tension created between thinking of the self and thinking of the other leads to a balance in the interaction that is profoundly equal and rewarding. Further, the recognition the child seeks is only possible because of the mother's independent identity. It is not something one can bring to oneself. Only another person can recognize one as an independent person of worth.

Benjamin stated:

> In this sense, notwithstanding the inequality between parent and child, recognition must be mutual and allow for the assertion of each self (p. 24).

There are of course many things that can go wrong in this scenario. The balance, for example, may be destroyed by a mother who is too distant (abandoning), too controlling, or both. When the balance is destroyed. The baby then loses the opportunity of feeling united and attuned as well as knowing the mother. In short, the child is never able to engage or disentangle from this predicament.

> In an ideal balance, a person is able to be
> fully self-absorbed or fully receptive to the
> other, he is able to be alone or together. In
> a negative cycle of recognition, a person
> feels that aloneness is only possible by
> obliterating the intrusive other, that attune-
> ment is only possible by surrendering to the
> other (Ibid, p. 28).

The failure of this early mutuality precludes the development of a more permeable boundary between the self and
others and results instead in the development of a defensive
boundary between the self and what is outside the self—
thus damaging the capacity for later erotic life and rewarding resonant relationships. Such persons may be seen to be
relegated to an interaction with other surfaces, not other
thinking, feeling people.

The conflict between assertion of the self and the recognition of the other was considered by Hegel (see Stace, 1955)
in his discussion of the master-slave relationship. Here, the
self's wish for absolute independence clashes with its need
for recognition. According to Hegel, the tension between
recognition and self-assertion must break down. Thus one
either dominates or is dominated. Recognition requires one
to be able to find oneself more or less accurately represented in the mind of the other.

The act of overpowering or dominating another erases the
opportunity for that other to recognize one's self in return.

Conversely if the other dominates, one's own self is erased and reduced to compliance with the other. In either case domination erases resonant equality.

A child raised in a context of domination will learn that interactions are by their nature asymmetrical. That is, someone must win, and someone must lose. This will seem to be the very nature of reality, as it is all the child has experienced.

Winnicott (1992) spoke of the process he called "destroying the object." In this view reality is not imposed from without but discovered from within. If the infant becomes enraged, for example, the infant will want to consume everything in its rage. It doesn't care. It has been hurt, and it wants to hurt back. If the parents are able to remain calm in the face of this rage, the infant is able to see the parents are able to survive its destruction. What is destroyed is the infant's notion that the parents would be destroyed by the rage (i.e., the internalized object of the parents). In this way, the infant is able to move beyond the internal object and discover the external reality. This opens the passage to interpersonal relating.

In such a situation the infant is able to "be with" the parent in a kind of "co-feeling" which allows for the sharing of emotions and intentions without demanding control as well as experiencing sameness without erasing difference.

When such development breaks down, the infant is threatened by dependency, as that impedes independence, and is also threatened by independence, as that precludes recognition.

Shaw (2010) suggested that clinically significant narcissism involves a failure to adequately develop a mode of empathic intersubjective relatedness. This state of affairs is the result of "cumulative relational trauma." Such trauma involves the infant's attempts to connect with a narcissistic parent who is incapable of relating equally.

To avoid this trauma, as argued by Bernstein (1992), both the self and the other must "stand under the reciprocal obligation to seek to transcend their narcissistic egoism." Benjamin (2004) similarly argued that the alternative to intersubjective recognition and relating is asymmetry, the domination and submission dynamic of doer and done-to (as described by Hegel above). In asymmetry one insists on the supremacy of one's own subjectivity and seeks to avoid becoming a victim of the other.

In this matrix the child is brought up to believe he or she can never win by a parent who exhibits "unyielding infallibility." Any opposition from the child earns punishment or the withdrawal of the parent's love and its replacement by contempt. Here the psychic survival of the child is at stake. This is the case as the parents lay claim to exclusive rights to goodness, innocence, purity, and perfection, whereas the child is the locus of badness.

The dominance and asymmetry of one subjectivity over the other becomes the model for relationships with significant others. The child subsequently does unto others as was done unto him or her. That is he or she is always right or good, and the other is always wrong or bad.

Clinically significant narcissists may be seen to be obsessed with maintaining a rigid sense of superiority, self-sufficiency, and entitlement (Shaw, Ibid). Such a sense is routinely delusional. Such persons learned as children that dependency is either contemptible or dangerous, as such things were disowned and ridiculed by the narcissistic parent. Avoiding a sense of dependency or shame by the use of the manic defense propels the pathological narcissist.

As a result the child of narcissistic parents has his or her identity formed by the parent not the self. That is the self is defined by the other and includes a sense of shameful badness.

Here the parent appears relentlessly superior. This guise is maintained as any sense of inadequacy is defended against at all cost as inadequacy is linked to a sense of shame. This shame is the result of cumulative trauma and shaming during the parent's development. Such parents, in other words, shame their children's legitimate dependency needs.

It is the asymmetrical nature of the environment in which such a child grows that does major damage to all subsequent relationships. Since for such a child, mutually equal empathic resonance is unknown, the only option is either to be on top or on the bottom, that is either to dominate or submit. Further, being on top is better. This kind of adjustment makes genuine equal-to-equal connection impossible.

Asymmetry is apparent in what is known as the dark triad: Machiavellianism, narcissism, and psychopathy. In these cases a person seeks to control the context instead of empathically connecting with it. Thus these are major areas in which domination is sought.

The matrix is sweetened in the case of bullies. Here an internal sense of inadequacy is covered by a gross display of external swagger and threat (i.e, reaction-formation). Domination is clearly the goal. Violence is possible in arranging or maintaining this position. If the bully is a parent, the child's self-affirming attempts are met with attack.

How common is this?

DeVega (2020) wrote:

> Tens of millions of Americans, at least, simply do not care about democracy or "the institutions." Approximately 20 percent of Americans are strong authoritarians. Many tens of millions are white supremacists and racists. Likewise, tens of millions of Americans support putting nonwhite migrants and refugees in…concentration camps.

Many people are the products of school systems that don't teach critical thinking skills, citizenship, or social skills. Many others feel alienated, lonely, fearful, and dissevered from social and political life. This leaves people unable to act due to despair, rage, or a struggle to simply survive.

Part of the background for this struggle may be traced to neoliberal economic policies that have long governed our society. These policies have led to massive inequalities (i.e., asymmetry) in wealth, income, and power that have expanded wildly since 1970. Such policies have also waged destructive assaults on the welfare state as well as the ecosystem (Giroux, 2020).

In this light it may be said the coronavirus crisis is more than a medical crisis. It is also a political and ideological crisis. Years of neoliberal thinking has denied the importance of public health and public well-being while at the same time defunding organizations that make these things possible. All of this plays out against a scenario of almost incomprehensible wealth-disparity and a crisis in democratic education, literacy, and social values.

In the neoliberal view, the markets should not only control trade but all aspects of the society. This view devalues the public sphere, the social contract, and public values, replacing these with unbounded self-interest and privatization. There is a strong condemnation of the public good. In this view individual interests are the only thing that matters, and those interests are purely monetary.

It is this philosophy, which has been adopted by corporate elites and wealthy influencers, that has increasingly guided events in American capitalism and society. The unopposed accumulation of wealth has been sanctioned over broad based social concern. Those who hold wealth support the dismantling of government checks and balances on maximum accumulations. Because these people have such power, they have been able to sway government to their cause.

Media platforms have been developed to broadcast endless falsehoods and misrepresentations in an effort to cast reality in terms that destabilize order and scientific evidence and instead support the views of the neoliberal rich. Hyper-capitalism has waged war on democracy and the public good for much of the past four decades.

Such a position easily emboldens fascism. Churchwell (see Giroux, Ibid) said:

> American fascist energies today are different from 1930s European fascism, but that doesn't mean they're not fascist, it means they're not European and it's not the 1930s. They remain organized around the classic fascist tropes of nostalgic regeneration, fantasies of racial purity, celebration of an authentic folk and nullification of others, scapegoating groups for economic instability or inequality, rejecting the legitimacy of political opponents, the demonization of critics, attacks on a free press, and claims that the will of the people justifies violent imposition of military force.

The coronavirus disaster has exposed several results of hyper-capitalism and right-wing policies. The effects of the virus are disproportionately in evidence among the disabled, the homeless, the poor, children, people of color, as well as essential workers and hospital staff (Ibid).

The conflict between the good of the many versus the good of the few defines the American dilemma.

Neoliberalism is related to narcissism in this way. Neoliberalism holds that the market should govern not only the market but all aspects of society. In other words the only thing that matters is money. If the market is in charge then the well-being of ordinary people ceases to be a focus. Since this is the case, government is often seen as the enemy as government routinely has different ends. These include social equality, justice, and democracy.

In short such a system renders most people superfluous as it does the planet itself. Education is enlisted in the cause of replacing human value with economic value. A consequence of this is a diminution of respect for truth, evidence, logic, and science and a replacement of these by a kind of fundamentalist epistemology that relies on mystification and resulting ignorance. Here thinking is replaced by feeling, and irrationality is common.

Wealthy corporations and media conglomerates create identities defined only by market values, i.e., themselves. What is good for these entities, however, is not so good for ordinary citizens. When medical systems primarily focus on monetary issues and profit, for example, they do not primarily focus on healing. We now live in a time when economic activity is dissevered from social costs.

Further, Giroux (Ibid) wrote:

The economic brutality and barbarism of neoliberal capital has joined with the forces of white supremacy and white nationalism to create an updated form of neoliberal fascism.

In this system inequality is a toxin that destroys lives, governmental systems, and civic culture. It robs people of a sense of agency and worth and contributes to their feelings of being helpless and impotent. In shifting away from a sense of individual worth and dignity, such a system emerges as a direct threat to democracy.

Hand in hand with the neoliberal opposition to widespread human welfare, the rise of Christian Nationalism has expanded in the U.S.

There exists a well-funded network of churches, non-profits, universities, think-tanks, and media outlets with direct lines to political officials (Theoharis, 2020). The message has been simple: God loves White Christian America and favors small government and big business. In this system it is people of Color as well as immigrants and the chronically poor who are blamed for society's ills.

Fundamentalist Christian influence is not new in the U.S. Segregationists used biblical phrases to enforce Jim Crow practices. The Moral Majority emphasized fundamentalist principles. Thessalonians was quoted as proof God supports work-requirements for public assistance.

In each of these cases biblical admonitions to help the poor have been turned around to support the wealthy and powerful. Today poverty is often seen as the result of bad behavior, laziness, or sin instead of the result of monetary manipulations by those in power. Further, it is commonly held in the "Bible Belt" that the poorest of White people are "better" than Black people simply because they are white.

The Bible, however interpreted, influences the daily lives of millions. This occurs in a country that has the resources at hand to end poverty, hunger, homelessness, and untold suffering but lacks the political will to do so (Ibid). In fact the political will is often the opposite. States that have passed voter suppression laws, those with the highest poverty rates, those that have not expanded Medicaid, and those who have passed anti-LGBTQ laws are also the states that have the highest concentrations of evangelical Protestants (Ibid).

Belief, of course, works differently than knowledge. Knowledge requires proof to back up its claims. Belief, on the other hand, can be held about anything. By lifting belief above knowledge, opinion is reified. This removes issues from the arena of checks and balances. It makes issues harder to contest. When rationality is relegated to second place in a culture, that culture loses its ties to the ground.

This is the danger of fundamentalist epistemology. It evades the rigor of rationality. When critical thinking is not taught in schools, the balance shifts to belief as that is easier to maintain and defend. When all knowledge is considered to be merely opinion, the ability to know reality is compromised. Such fine points may be lost on a population that is largely unable to read and comprehend the daily newspaper.

Indeed, education is difficult for some. Many of these people must seek income via the use of labor. That the educated class has been able to exploit these people is seen in the steadily increasing disparity of wealth. Steverman and Tanzi (2020) reported that fifty U.S. individuals hold as much wealth as the poorest 165 million Americans combined.

The differential in wealth goes hand in hand with a differential in power. This is especially true when one's group is threatened with a loss of standing in the system. When computers and robots are able to displace many strong backs, the strong-back community is threatened. When the majority of resources flow to the people of knowledge, fewer resources remain for the people of strength.

None of these situations necessarily bring about polarity. To result in polarity, an asymmetrical interaction is also required. There must be a group seeking to dominate others.

Such a group is the combination of White Christian fundamentalism and corporate power that has had great success in the U.S. This system is now firmly entrenched in the management of millions of people. The two areas feed each other and suggest the capitalist system is "God driven." Political polarity results as this group seeks to dominate and control those who largely favor the equality outlined by democracy.   Allowing each person an equal voice is antithetical to allowing a small number of people to control the lives and welfare of citizens.

When the voices of ordinary people are muffled, only the voices in power matter. When power, wealth, and approved belief systems are what matter human dignity, empathy, and honest reaction cease to matter. Millions upon millions of Americans are swayed by the voices of power to ignore their own welfare. Power has become intoxicating to those who have little of it as the pursuit of power masks the pitiful quality of their own lives.

Such a polarized struggle routinely ignores considerations of mental health. Power matters more than mental health, and, as the saying goes, wealth is the road to happiness. But wealth and power are little without healthy mental functioning. Such claims are routinely ignored. The system demands consumers. Buying something is the cure for all ills. And we must keep buying instead of seeking to improve ourselves by improving the quality of our functioning and our interpersonal relationships.

Only when all people are considered to be of equal worth as human beings does equality obtain. Asymmetrical interactions result in dominance and submission. If I can sleep well-fed and easy while a third of the city doesn't have enough to eat, enough for needed medical treatment, enough to pay the rent, I am a person deaf to the human condition.

The notion of domination, however, requires further understanding. Foucault (See Foucault and Gordon, 1980) claimed:

> If power were never anything but repressive, if it never did anything but say no, do you really think one would be brought to obey it?

In Foucault's understanding power does not deny desire but forms it "converting it into a willing retainer, its servant or representative (Benjamin, Ibid)." Seen in this way domination as a system transforms all elements of the psyche. In this view obedience to the laws of the society is not brought about by fear but by love. If our relationship is good, we as children love our parents who have requirements of us. Learning to obey when it is appropriate is an important social and interpersonal skill.

What this means is that domination involves a two-way agreement: one person dominates, and the other submits. A change in this agreement by either party upsets the equation.

In the famous chapter from The Brothers Karamazov (originally published 1879-1880) entitled The Grand Inquisitor, Dostoyevsky took up the topic of domination. In this telling Ivan Karamazov is speaking to his brother Alyosha, who is a priest. Ivan spins a tale of Christ who has returned to earth during the Inquisition and confronts the Inquisitor about the church's corruption of the faith. He asks, in short, why has a spontaneous act of love been transformed into submission?

The Inquisitor answers that the people don't want freedom or truth as these things only bring suffering and require courage. What people want instead is miracle, mystery, and authority. The pain that attends compliance, he says, is less than the pain that attends freedom. It is the authority of the church, he holds, that makes pain bearable. It is this authority and its attendant hope for redemption that inspires voluntary submission. Thus fear and adoration are fused by a hope of reward.

The Inquisitor rebukes the image of Christ for sending people into the world with "some promise of freedom which men in their simplicity and their natural unruliness cannot even understand, which they fear and dread—for nothing has ever been more insupportable for a man and a human society than freedom." (p. 262).

Freedom is frightening as one must rely on oneself and the resources he or she can muster. Such efforts could come to naught, and one would be left with no support.

The Inquisitor continues:

> "Feed men, and then ask of them virtue!"
> that's what they'll write on the banner,
> which they will raise against You, and with
> which they will destroy Your temple (Ibid).

Psychoanalytically, domination begins in the attempt to deny dependency. The child wants independence from the mother upon whom he or she is dependent. Yet achieving this independence is not enough. The child's independence must be recognized by the mother upon whom he has been dependent. Independence and recognition form a circle that requires a tension between self-needs and other-needs in order to be successful. When this system breaks down, there is only domination. If I dominate you, I erase you. If you dominate me, you erase me.

In this view the tension formed between recognition and independence allows both parties to be present. When this tension fails, on the other hand, the need for recognition is transformed into domination.

The denial of dependency in the modern world requires considerable effort and resource. People are dependent on the money they make in order to buy food. They are dependent on government to keep them safe at night, collect their garbage, educate their children, just as they are dependent on others to fix their cars, computers, appliances, plumbing, &c. Dependence on the health care system is profound.

Dependency goes hand in hand with a fear of that which is beyond one's control. This is especially true if one's life has consisted of a battle with others for domination.

These are not issues that are easy to solve, if, in fact, they are even solvable. Clearly the problems of capitalism are acute. Reining in the unfettered greed of the few in the service of improving better lives for millions of other citizens is, as they say, a no-brainer. Allowing the healthcare system to free itself from dominant business management policies will enable it focus more on healing and less on profit for a few owners.

One issue that will not be easy to manage is sadism. We have enjoyed hurting the other guys—those with whom we disagree. We have hoped for their destruction. We want to punish them as we have been punished. We want to enact revenge. We have identified with our own aggressors. What will become of our anger, our hate? Will we develop the ability to bring it home, or will we continue to project it outward onto others?

For these and other reasons, the problems we are facing require a consideration of mental health. Narcissism with its asymmetrical pattern is not an example of good mental and emotional functioning. It is, in fact, a disorder. The wish to profit at the expense of others requires a profound failure of empathy.

It also suggests an emotionally traumatic childhood in which empathy was missing. There are tens of millions of American citizens who are treated this way every day. We have not found a way to teach them to read or bring them adequate health care let alone help them to develop empathy.

Nonetheless, a society that holds as a central value the concern for all people is a different society than one that holds wealth and power as its central value. The scales have tipped too far. It is the people themselves who matter.

REFERENCES

Benjamin, J. The Bonds of Love: Psychoanalysis, Feminism, and the Problem of Domination. Pantheon, 1988.

Benjamin, J. Beyond Doer and Done To: An Intersubjective View of Thirdness. Psychoanalytic Quarterly, 73, pp. 5-46.

Bernstein, R. The New Constellation. MIT Press, 1992.

DeVega, C. Trump and his movement are evil—but the hope-peddlers in the chattering class won't say so. Salon, 09-27-2020.

Dostoyevsky, F. The Brothers Karamazov. Suzeteo, 2018.

Foucault, M. and Gordon, C. (Ed.) Power/Knowledge:Selected Interviews and Other Writings, 1972-1977. Vintage, 1980.

Giroux, H.A. Dystopian plagues and fascist politics in the age of Trump: Finding hope in the darkness. Salon, 10-04, 2020.

Scamainaci, J. III Battle with Bullets: Advancing a Vision of Civil War. https://www.politicalresearch.org/2020/08/31/battle-bullet-advancing-vision-civil-war

Shaw, D. Enter Ghosts: The Loss of Intersubjectivity in Clinical Work with Adult Children of Pathological Narcissists. Psychoanalytic Dialogues, 20, 2010, pp. 46-59.

Stace, W.T. The Philosophy of Hegel. Dover, 1955.

Steverman, B., and Tanzi, A. The 50 Richest Americans are Worth as Much as the Poorest 165 Million. Bloomberg, 10-08-2020.

Theoharis, L. The rise of Christian Nationalism in America. Solon, 10-04, 2020.

Winnicott, D.W. The Child, the Family and the Outside World. Perseus, 1992.

AFTERWORD

The task we face, after the chaos and destruction of the Trump years, is putting the country back together. Layers of stultifying autocratic sludge have gummed up everything to which authority could lay claim. This must be changed into operations headed by non-authoritarian facilitators. The problem of narcissistic development must be made visible to all, and measures must be taken to reduce the incidence of its formation. We must heal the culture.

It will require each of us to recognize and grieve our own contributions to the problem. If we do not do this, we will continue to blame others, and there will be no healing. Not all issues are black or white as in binary thinking. More complex thought is required to successfully manage reality and the rebuilding of a diverse culture.

Narcissism, greed and power, both at the hands of the educated and uneducated, have brought America to its lowest point. Our country needs to be redirected toward becoming a fair and equitable society for all. We must reclaim a cooperative place in the world of nations. Academics and scientists must be heard. Each of us must become a member of the group of human beings who care about each other instead of insular beings only interested in ourselves. Psychological advances in parenting and the developmental processes must be made widely available, and the health-care and mental-health systems must be open to all people regardless of means.

There is an old saying that if you are a hammer, everything looks like a nail. That is you come up with a solution in terms of where you stand. As American culture struggles to become more developed and humane, it must move beyond using force to solve all of its problems.

Smoldering racial feelings have guided too many for too long. The moneyed class has brutalized the working class and gotten away with it. Everyone must be heard. There must be an end to the dumbing-down of the culture and the consequent opposition to study and learning.

It is time for a new beginning, a new chapter. The American culture must find a way to extend justice for all, not just for the rich and powerful, not just for those in charge, not just for political entities, but for all Americans.

We must find a way to include each other, or we will per-ish.

This means finding a way to talk with those who won't listen. It means finding a place for those one opposes. It means placing a value on tolerance and inclusion. Each of us remember someone in our childhood who was kind and tried to help us. How this person stood out! How different he or she was from the others! And how long we have re-membered him or her and been thankful.

Despite our culture, it is not all about us. It is, rather, about all-of-us. When what is good for me is bad for you, the equation needs to be rethought. Even trying to be a re-sponsible and caring person can enhance the whole block. It may not change the world, but it improves the block. Be-ing a parent children can love is a big deal. Being a parent who cares, who hears, and who is present changes the world. At least here.

The survival of the American project requires us to learn to give something back to the cultural fabric. We have to learn to work for America in addition to working for our-selves. All people means *all* people. It starts with each one of us.